Slay the Dragons — Free the Genie

Moving past negativity and resistance
to get great results

Bennett A. Neiman, Ph.D.

Illustrated by George Willett

Illustrator of "Whack On The Side of The Head"
and "Kick In The Seat Of The Pants'

Chrysalis Publications

Slay The Dragons – Free the Genie
Copyright ©2004 by Dr. Bennett A. Neiman

For information, please address:
Chrysalis Publishing
133 Whitney Dr.
Woodstock, NY 12498
845-679-7072
chrysalis-consulting.com

Library of Congress Cataloging-in-Publication Data

Neiman, Bennett A.
Slay the Dragons – Free the Genie

ISBN #0-9747357-0-1

Illustrated by George Willett

Cover by Paul Maring

---

10 9 8 7 6 5 4 3 2 1

Author's Preface

How many deadly dull meetings have you suffered through in your work, school or church? Why does so much useless energy go into defending turf instead of building a common vision? Even when people are really jazzed after meetings, how come they often drag their feet—then get exasperated when little gets done?

Breakdowns abound where *any* group with differing agendas and personalities converge, but the worst problems occur when something truly important is being planned, like a key project, an annual operating plan or a long-term strategic plan. Guarded and leery of negative interactions, people talk about the agenda but are actually mired in turf, insecurity and past pain. New ideas and motivation get squelched when the naysayers move in. Brainstorming often degenerates into habitual limiting assumptions—and few dare to dream big.

For a long time I wrestled with the central question: how can leaders slay the dragons that suck the life out of their organizations or teams—and free the genie that ignites great collaborations? So, over the past nine years I have co-created, learned and developed various tools and techniques to re-focus, re-inspire, and revitalize groups.

After years of doing these kinds of programs, and continuously being asked if there were any books that supported these ideas, I realized that there was a hole in the human resources and organizational development literature, and wrote this book.

Though developed for internal facilitators and leaders who run corporate planning processes (like Six Sigma Black Belts), this book is a powerful tool for any kind of meeting. It is for people who have never heard of Six Sigma: for leaders, managers, trainers and facilitators. The ideas and techniques introduced can be used in newly merged divisions, warring factions, teams stuck in habitual patterns, well-meaning community groups who never reach closure—even families facing big decisions together. Its concepts and clear exercises can help turn <u>any</u> planning or decision-making meeting into a productive, inspiring event.

This book *will not* cover the basics of meeting management; there are already plenty of those books out there. Nor is it yet another book on team building. Instead, this book addresses a larger convergence of strategic planning, visioning and creative thinking.

Slay the Dragons — Free the Genie goes beyond theory and offers exciting practical tools to rally the troops. Breaking through entrenched cultures, this approach does in 1-2 day seminars what often hasn't been addressed in years.

In this book you'll meet the six dragons that suck the life out of organizations:

➤ Blah-blah Blob
➤ Unspeakable Ugly
➤ Political Chicken
➤ Idea Eater
➤ Chattering Monkey
➤ Well-Meaning Weasel

Through *Slay the Dragons — Free the Genie*, you'll gain 27 specific dragon-slayers to help make any meeting better, easier, more effective, faster and more enjoyable. Some of the ideas introduced will appear slightly unorthodox, and at times I will ask you to stretch beyond your comfort zone. It should be worth it — thousands who have done this work attest that it works!

Armed with the tools, techniques and ideas introduced in *Slay the Dragons — Free the Genie*, you'll learn to:

• Understand the hidden group dynamics of meetings and planning sessions and how they can undermine your agenda

- Guide your participants to a new way of looking at themselves and their organization

- Spark creative, out-of-the-box thinking that fuels innovation and discovery

- Create a cohesive group atmosphere that moves past cynicism and is re-dedicated to addressing key bottom line issues

- Create consensus on how to best execute the agenda and build in easy accountability for the life of your plan, if planning is involved

Employing these techniques, you will see people *at all levels*, stretching, dreaming and reinventing themselves and their organizations. Six Sigma and other leaders and facilitators will spearhead new solutions that uncover hidden waste and shake up the culture. Even skeptics will stop accepting the status quo and *go for the brass ring*.

You in?

Dr. Ben Neiman
Woodstock, New York

Acknowledgements

To Michelle Fogle and Jon McKenzie, coordinators of Texas Instruments' (formerly Motorola's) Six Sigma Soft Skills Survival Camp, who first took a chance on me and believed in my team innovation and creative planning processes.

To Tracy Cox, Dave Oberholtzer and the other Raytheon Six Sigma Navigators who deserve ample credit for nurturing my Visionary Team Planning process at the onset and tailoring it specifically for the Six Sigma Black Belt community.

And to my wife, Chris Neiman, a fine management consultant in her own right, who devoted so many hours helping me to craft a bunch of concepts and far-flung experiences into this book.

Special Thanks

To my editor and friend, Marianne Fleischer, and the people who graciously gave important editorial input to this book: Andy Lee, Donna Andujo, Michelle Fogle, Neal Mackertich, Geoff Bannister, Gwen Krause, Roseann Hartfield, Christine Tricoli, Carol Schneider and Marc Lewis.

Forward by Tracy Cox,
Six Sigma Master Black Belt

I first encountered the "mad man" who is Dr. Ben Neiman in 1995 at a Six Sigma Black Belt workshop in Austin, Texas. We were there to hone our statistical and problem-solving skills. Little did I know then that Dr. Ben, as thousands now call him, would bring an entirely fresh perspective to the notion of organizational change. He inspires teams to go beyond what they believe possible as a group and facilitate a personal change begun in the heart.

Slay the Dragons — Free the Genie is a culmination of Dr. Ben's life, work and passion. To break it down into its component parts, you will find visioning, strategic and team planning, team building, creative thinking, sponsorship, brainstorming, and loads of fun and humor. I discovered something after nine years of working with Dr. Ben and facilitating this fantastic technology over and over again: The "free the genie" part goes beyond the actual learning. Something magical happens that transforms people as they awaken to the entire process.

I have had the pleasure of using this process and technology as a Six Sigma Master Black Belt with teams of vice presidents, directors, engineers, human resources representatives, information technology professionals, and many more at all levels of an organization. Did it work every time? Of course not with every soul. Was the result extremely positive? Yes!

In fact, Raytheon Company now trains all new Six Sigma Experts (or Black Belts) in the techniques of Visionary Team Planning as part of their core training. It is being used in every business and organization of our Company with great results. Simply stated, employing these tools and techniques over time can change your organization's entire culture.

So if, at first blush, you are skeptical about how this "crazy stuff" will be received by leaders in your company, believe me, they will not only receive it well, *your* team's stock will rise for bringing it into the organization. Enjoy the ride and set your sights for something wonderful, because dragons *will* be slain and the genie *will* come out of the lamp!

Tracy Cox

Contents

Introduction: Once Upon A Time in Corporateland

Once upon a time there was a rich kingdom, called Corporateland, full of hope, bold ventures and fat bonuses. The castle staff drew top talent, including a Magic Genie. Daringly resourceful, charismatic, and creative to his core, this Genie inspired others to go for gold.

When the river threatened to flood Corporateland, the Genie organized people and built a dam, then used the hydropower to light the palace. When the court fell ill to a bad cut of mutton or lost their tunics in iffy junk bonds, the Genie would say, "Sometimes you win, and sometimes you learn!"

There were three vitality centers that were powerful symbols of the kingdom's glory and success. They were "The Roundtable of Collaboration," "The Magic Cauldron of Innovation," and "The Tower of Vision." These seats of power were particularly dear to the inhabitants of Corporateland, and their presence inspired hope and confidence in all.

Under the Genie's golden influence, the kingdom prospered. The word on the shire was "This is a cool place to work." Though fear and stonings raged at other castles, collaboration, innovation and vision were business-as-usual here.

During yet another reorg, members of the High Council became nervous about defending their status quo. "With our high profile," they reasoned, "surely some SOB rival will try a hostile takeover. Let's not jeopardize our 401Ks by taking unnecessary risks. You know, the Dark Ages weren't that long ago!"

"Yes, no risks," middle managers parroted in unison. "Suppose locusts eat our crops? Suppose the townspeople opt for another coin of the realm? We must sit tight," they squeaked, as fear squashed their drive and joy.

Despite the Genie's loud and repeated protests, the Council decided strong restrictions should be instituted. Six fire-breathing dragons were brought in to guard the kingdom's prosperity and stalk troublemakers. Two dragons were placed at each of the power centers, The Roundtable of Collaboration, The Magic Cauldron of Innovation, and The Tower of Vision. Anyone who dared challenge the dragons was attacked.

The Genie was furious. "What are you doing?" he bellowed. "It's the wrong strategy: fear will kill our spirit. If our crops fail, we will grow new ones! If our jealous neighbors come, we will negotiate win-win partnerships over a series of power lunches!"

"That's enough, Genie. Your simplistic ways are for children," the Council decreed. "Don't you see, there could be danger. We are men of great standing. We have responsibilities to shareholders and analysts."

Then the word spread to intranets hither and yon, "If you dare disturb the status quo, you might as well redo your resume."

So the Genie was locked in the castle dungeon, the castle staff hunkered down, and six dragons stalked the land.

Each power center was taken over by two of the six dragons.

The two dragons stationed at the Round Table of Collaboration, made certain that no collaboration happened. One got in the way so people couldn't work together and the other made sure it wasn't a safe place to speak your mind or tell the truth.

One of the dragons stationed at the Magic Cauldron of Innovation saw to it that everyone stayed politically correct and way in-the-box. The other one ate up any new ideas that tried to get out.

And the dragons over at the Tower of Vision kept the people short-sighted and made certain they didn't follow-through on their dreams or meet their commitments.

Without the Genie, the people in Corporateland lost confidence in their ability to create.

Worse still, when the village analysts heard that the court was losing its talent edge, they went elsewhere looking for the *next big thing*.

Sound familiar?

* * *

Freeing the Group Genie

Many organizations in America, whether corporations, governments, schools, religious institutions, social service agencies, or community associations, have unwittingly loosed their dragons and stuffed their genie into a bottle. So many organizations begin with the same entrepreneurial zeal the Genie possessed; fueled by a sense of infinite possibility, they exude hope that instills confidence in others. They launch with a fiery commitment to excellence, which is maintained by creativity, fun and communal purpose.

They start out truly embodying the three key characteristics of vitality that enable organizations to thrive: collaboration, innovation, and visioning. Yet, over time, they care more about preserving security and less about the very lifeblood that is their organization's reason for being. Not losing becomes more important than fully winning. They start making small, measured decisions that maximize safety and minimize experimentation and novelty.

The result: a sound, gray existence that protects business-as-usual, but squelches the child-like sense of wonder that brings out the creative genie in us all. With the collective genie imprisoned, the inspired initiative that ignites a successful company is also imprisoned.

Yes, the fire is out, so the house can't burn down.

Yet neither can the fire warm its people, light up the community — or the world.

What's Next

The deadly serious dynamics that are a *"drag on"* meetings and planning sessions everywhere (or for shorthand, **The Dragons**) delight in keeping teams from collaboration, innovation and a common vision. In the next section, we'll examine those dragons one by one:

- Blah-blah Blob
- Idea Eater
- Unspeakable Ugly
- Political Chicken
- Chattering Monkey
- Well-Meaning Weasel

This book will take you on a journey to recover the vitality centers, slay a few dragons and maybe have some fun.

Chapter 1: The Roundtable of Collaboration: Freeing the Group Genie

"I not only use the brains I have, I use all the brains I can borrow."

-Woodrow Wilson

Best Practices cultures know that collaboration is at the core of team success. Lack of alignment is a key cause of low team vitality and lackluster innovation. Of course, what makes teams work or fail is too large a conversation for this book. Yet consider how true collaboration fuels productivity. Consider how the lack of it deflates morale and effectiveness. How do we reclaim the Collaboration Roundtable for our organizations?

Real-Life Fairy Tales

A well-meaning and competent CIO headed a department of hard-working employees at a fair-sized consulting firm in Philadelphia. Like teams everywhere, they had staff meetings every two weeks. These awful meetings were the bane of the staff's existence. Grandstanding, endless off-point storytelling and lax meeting management dragged these sessions into three-hour endurance contests. This created such frustration that rude interrupting, tuning-out and negativity were rampant. The only thing creative about these meetings was the ways in which employees competed with each other to AVOID them!

At a highly successful chemical company based Connecticut, a similar story was unfolding. For several years a brilliant, award-winning R&D team developed an amazing number of patented products. All was well until some marketing VP alerted the leader that none of these inventions actually made it to market—or made money!

So a commercialization team was created, merging the R&D group with a marketing group, under the leadership of the marketing director. The novel idea was to create products that would *actually sell*. Yet the two groups were so different and so protective of their own ways that conflict and righteous indignation flared on both sides. The fast-talking marketing wizards alienated the R&D geniuses, who in turn became passive-aggressive. After two years of meetings, they were still at square one.

Alignment's Effect On Collaboration

What we are talking about here is the human tendency to get out of sync. It is a corporate phenomenon that smart, well-meaning, competent people often get together in meetings and end up creating results that are neither smart nor useful.

This is a question of alignment, plain and simple. The point of meetings is *not* to convert people to another way of thinking, nor to get everybody to salute the same flag. The idea is to get the group to agree on a good game plan they can live with. The following two big arrows illustrate:

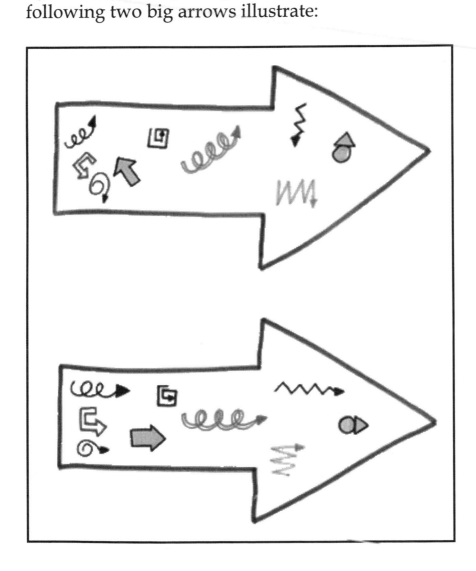

In the first vector, we have squirrelly characters with different shapes and sizes, all pointed in different directions. Like a group of different personalities with different skills and no common direction, this arrow isn't going anywhere. The second vector has the same squirrelly characters. None of them change their sizes. None of them change their shapes. They retain their individuality, their personality and their unique characters. Yet now they are lined up in the same direction. This second arrow is going somewhere!

An effective team process does not try to change the personalities or values of the people involved. It moves people in the same direction, which, in turn, can move mountains.

It's Sort of Like Basketball

Imagine a basketball team facing a big game with the cross-town rival. Someone says, "Okay, how do we beat these guys?" A guard says, "Oh, I know this team well. To beat them we need to play an offensive, run-and-shoot, fast-paced game. We'll fast-break on every play and take lots of three-point shots. Both teams will score over 100 points, but we'll run them ragged. And that's how to beat 'em."

Nearly everyone nods their head. But one of the forwards says, "No, wait a minute. I used to play with these guys. That's the opposite of what we should do. We have to slow the ball down, press on both sides of the court and keep both scores under 60 points. A defensive struggle is how we beat them!"

Who is right? Who knows—on any given day, either of them could be right! Yet one thing is certain: before the team members go out on the court, they have to agree to play the same game. If some of the guys play a defensive game and others play an offensive game, they'll surely lose.

Now if you are that basketball forward and begrudgingly go along with the majority, you might say, "Hey, I still think I'm right. And if we lose this game, I'm telling you, you're going to hear from me. And the next time we're going to do it my way." That's okay. The main thing is to create a direction that's going to work for the whole group. That means some may have to give up some things and others will bend at other times. That's alignment and what creates a sense of collaboration. And true collaboration means team effectiveness and power.

And the Moral of the Story Is...

So how did the consulting team at that Philadelphia firm deal with the bloated meetings? At our suggestion, they tried having meetings standing up. Yes, standing up!

This unorthodox method produced stellar results: the meetings were never longer than 45 minutes and negativity, interrupting, and storytelling dropped dramatically. At the end of four months, the team decided that it understood the group dynamics well enough to sit down again and with their newly acquired skills kept the meetings short and to-the-point.

What became of the warring marketing geniuses and R&D scientists up in Connecticut? The members of both groups took off for two days to air their grievances and in a thorough and non-confrontational way, made new agreements and commitments. As a result, the team was re-energized and soon took three successful new products to market.

Bring Back the Roundtable!

It's time to up the alignment of your group, but—beware—there are two lurking dragons, Blah-blah Blob and Unspeakable Ugly, that will be guarding the gate to the Roundtable of Collaboration. The next two sections will give you several tools to face these dragons with confidence.

The First "Drag on" Collaboration: Blah-blah Blob

*"Most of what we say and do is unnecessary —
choose your words and actions wisely."*

- Marcus Aurelius

Observable Symptoms:

- The meeting is bloated. Everyone is involved in every one of the many issues, so people become overwhelmed, bored and tune out.

- The whole group gets lost in a sea of wordsmithing or arguing and nothing is decided.

- The meeting drags on . . . forever.

The problem with so many meetings, particularly planning meetings, is that they are fat, stuffed, crowded and tedious. By fat, I mean that they are padded with circular discussions. Arguing, posturing and pontificating abound. This M.O. is not only unnecessary, it is seriously detrimental to healthy, efficient meetings.

Why do meetings get "fat"?

Some people come in with specific agendas or an axe to grind, while others just like to get on their soapbox and make their points *very, very, very* clear.

Some people just like to talk a lot and—hey—meetings are a good place to get heard.

Rarely is the leader of the meeting prepared for all of this, so the meeting drags on without closure and without important decisions being made.

Two levels of attack will help subdue this dragon:
- Address the structure of the meeting
- Do something about the individuals

In general, it's easier to work with the structure, which is what this section addresses. We will take on the individuals in the next section.

Obviously, good facilitators use good meeting management skills, have a game plan, a printed agenda, take frequent breaks, *etc.* However, *great* facilitators EXPECT that Blah-blah Blob will show up and are armed and ready with six powerful Dragon Slayers to knock this Dragon out of the meeting.

Dragon Slayer #1: Stand-up Kinda Guys

Whenever anyone says that their staff meetings are too long and boring and no one sticks to the agenda, I say, "Have standing meetings!" If you stand, no one will stray far from the agenda, because everyone will want the meeting to end soon. You can't stand more than 30 or 40 minutes, no matter what!

In an all-day planning meeting, people have to be able to sit down some of the time, but try to keep this to a minimum. Have them up on their feet, doing some team or individual challenge early in the day to get their blood, creativity and energy moving.

Dragon Slayer #2: Break It Up

Ever noticed that when a big group breaks into small units, the noise level and energy in the room change? Everyone who has run a meeting has had this experience: in the large group the group is moribund, dull-eyed, slack-jawed and . . . quiet. You ask a question and get some reluctant responses.

Yet break them up into small groups, give them a flip chart and the same question to answer, and they buzz away like bees. Soon they'll come back with a flip chart page filled with responses to the same question no one would speak up about minutes before.

Small groups have a much higher productivity rate than large ones. They are far better at avoiding uncomfortable group dynamics, like dominant participants and "group think" mentality.

Organizational development studies repeatedly show that when brainstorming, five people will do 90 per cent of what 25 people can do, usually in less time.

So if you have four issues to to discuss, it is more efficient to have small groups do the initial discussion and then present the conclusions to

> Small groups have much higher productivity rates.

the larger group. The larger group can then add the last 10 per cent—using much less time and with happier participants.

Studies show that the most effective small group size is five or six people. This is large enough for interesting conversation but not so large that some people can't easily participate. With a group of this size, you'll get good interaction with fewer of the non-productive dynamics that can sidetrack meetings.

Small groups are where the real work happens. Large groups are best for presentations followed by *brief* discussions, whole group decisions, specifically designed exercises and learning experiences.

If you try to do things in a large group that belong in a small group, the Blah-blah Blob will roll in and weigh down the experience.

Dragon Slayer #3: Carousel Brainstorming

Most of us have been frustrated by monologues and useless dialogues that seem to drag on forever when a group is trying to brainstorm ideas. Another common complaint is feeling railroaded by pushier types who seem to hog all the airtime. Though everyone comes to get something done, often these sessions degenerate into a series of speeches, with little if any productive outcome.

I was working with a city government in a small Alabama town. The diverse populations were openly hostile and predictably dug in their heels along racial lines. Like warring tribes or ancient fiefdoms, people held their ground and their entrenched positions. This city government desperately needed to reach consensus but that felt like the Impossible Dream to the participants.

So we used a powerful technique that helps *squeeze the fat* out of meetings and moves sticky issues along in a productive way. "Carousel Brainstorming" is a team-building and visioning tool that can also be YOUR secret weapon. It will produce efficient brainstorming in several areas and keep your meeting lean.

A Word about Post-its

Before I describe this secret weapon, let me say a word or two about Post-it notes. If you are not already using them in your brainstorming activities, I strongly suggest you give them a try. Whether working by yourself or with others, when you need to generate and organize ideas, Post-its will greatly enhance the process. The general idea is to print one idea on each Post-it (preferably with an easy-to-read pen, like a Vis-à-vis overhead marking pen) then lay the Post-its out (posting them on a flipchart or wall is the usual way to do this) and organize them until they make sense to you. This organizing, or "affinity grouping" will give you new insights and awarenesses.

How to Carousel Brainstorm

Back to our Dragon Slayer. If the group is getting together to brainstorm and discuss five different topics:

- Put the topics on five different flip chart pages around the room.

- Remind everyone of the rules: one idea per Post-it, print clearly, no discussion.

- Have all participants, armed with Post-it note pads and pens, "carousel" around the room putting their best thoughts or comments on each of the five charts. When they approach a chart, have them first read what has already been posted by others. Then have them put a check on the Post-it notes with which they strongly agree. If they have a new thought, they can add their own Post-it notes to the chart.

- After everyone has had a chance to contribute the initial information to all of the topics, assign a small group (we'll call them the "cluster group") to each chart.

- Instruct each cluster group to organize the information, *i.e.*, read through all the Post-it notes, cluster them into categories, name the categories and be prepared to report the essence of what has been said to the whole group.

- Finally, have a spokesperson from each cluster group report what's on the flip chart followed by a brief (and usually rich) discussion by the whole group. (Since this is the only discussion time, you must allow some free and lively conversation. Yet try to keep these rich discussions to a minimum or things will get out of hand.)

Carousel Brainstorming levels the playing field, so that the "quieter" people are heard as freely as the freely as the "noisy" ones. It generates rich data while avoiding common problems of grandstanding, digressions, side-tracking, dominant people hijacking the agenda, and quieter participants not being heard.

> Carousel Brainstorming levels the playing field, so that the "quieter" people are heard as freely as the "noisy" ones.

Carousel Brainstorming saved the day in that little town in Alabama. Finally *all* the voices could be heard equally without ruffling feathers or taking sides. After years of distrust, suddenly the townspeople were having a great time working together. With the in-fighting out of the way, they could see common interests. For the first time they could get past old bitter issues and work on their common future together.

Dragon Slayer #4: Dot Technology

It's amazing how powerful something so simple can be! Consider the humble dot.

In many meetings you will need to prioritize or simplify a list, for instance, a list of issues or possible strategies, solutions or action steps. One way to do this is to use colored dots to prioritize items on a flip chart. These small circular labels (found in any business supply store) easily peel off their sheets and stick to just about anything. Here's how "Dot Technology" works:

- Give each person some dots. As a rule of thumb, use three dots for every seven items on a list to prioritize. I usually make my list so that there are six or seven inches of space to the left for the dots to fit.

- Have participants "vote" for the items they feel are most important, critical, effective, or whatever measure is relevant, by placing their dots next to the items. When everyone steps back, the strong opinion of the overall group will be instantly evident.

The power of those little critters cannot be overstated. They cut through the rhetoric. They categorically show how much "juice" the group has about any given issue; whether there is a lot of energy or hardly any. Like Carousel Brainstorming, the humble dots democratically give everyone (the shy, the intimidated, the subordinate) the same voice.

Note that dot voting should be used as a barometer of the group opinion or energy, and not as a vote. Once the conversation gets underway, information may come out that will elevate an item to a higher priority, and of course team leaders will adjust. This fast prioritization exercise, however, will not have been wasted; you will have avoided the (unfortunately frequent) phenomenon of endless time spent discussing items of very little actual interest to the group, to the detriment of those that really are important.

Dots pair beautifully with Carousel Brainstorming. If the team needs a decision about a given topic/flip chart page, then everyone gets colored dots to "vote" for items on each flip chart. This prioritizes options for the final decision. Imagine how much time this saves, while semi-anonymously letting *all know* where the group stands as a whole.

Dragon Slayer #5: "Can You Live With It?"

In any decision-making session, there has to be give-and-take and collaboration to achieve real buy-in. When participants get obstinate and draw lines in the sand around given initiatives or ideas, progress stops. When people just "go along with" group decisions (out of a misplaced need for harmony, boredom, or an unwillingness to stand up for their beliefs) the result is equally deadening. This sabotages the process by limiting the full power of the group.

What cuts through this conundrum? Try a time-tested consensus model that ensures buy-in, moves things along and gains closure. We call it the "Can you live with it?" model. This could be introduced to your group with something like the following:

Reaching consensus could be a real bear, depending on which approach we use. For instance, if we use the "get everybody to love it" approach, it will take us two months to reach consensus. You and everybody will have different opinions and none of us are going to love everything decided today. Of course, you may love some of the things, like the things you worked on or proposed. But for sure you won't love everything, so the "everybody loves it" consensus model will not serve us.

Now, what if we tried to use the "we all like it" consensus model? It would still take two weeks. What we need is something more workable. So when it comes time to ask for group agreement, I will not say, "Do you love it?" or "Do you like it?" Instead, I will ask, "Can you live with it?" That means that, even if you are not totally crazy about it, you can support it.

Can you live with this consensus model?

Thumbthing that Helps

Once there is an agreement to be on-board with the "can you live with it" concept, you might want to use the "thumbs" method to test the consensus waters. Here's how it works: tell the participants that when an idea has been proposed, a thumb check will be taken. Everyone sticks a thumb in the air; thumbs up means "Yes!", thumbs down means "No!", and thumbs to the side means "I've got a concern or a question or I don't understand the proposal." So when you say, "Can I see thumbs on that?" the group will tell you quickly (and quietly!) what the general position is.

Obviously, this is a great gauge for the facilitator to determine how good a solution is. When there are a lot of sideways and/or down thumbs, the facilitator needs to back up and allow more discussion before pushing for consensus. On the other hand, when there is a sea of thumbs up and just a few downs or sideways, you can easily and quickly address the outstanding issues.

The "Can You Live with It" consensus model encourages alignment, it hits that Blah-blah Blob dragon where it hurts and brings you closer to the Collaboration Roundtable.

Dragon Slayer #6: Push To Closure

Time constraints are important in meetings because discussions tend to expand to fill the time allotted, and there is always so much to be discussed. People need clear boundaries to help them close out discussions.

> **Human nature being what it is, people in meetings would rather stay in the fun discussion phase, than in the hard decision phase.**

Human nature being what it is, people in meetings would rather stay in the (fun) discussion phase, than in the (hard) decision or closure phase. If you are facilitating, one of your important jobs is to keep steering the discussion toward closure.

Have you had trouble reaching closure from time to time in meetings you have been called upon to facilitate? If you have, you are not alone. I have been facilitating corporate meetings for over twenty-five years and I can tell you, some people go to extremes to keep meetings off track and off purpose.

To maximize the chances of a meeting you are facilitating being successful, I recommend you say something like the following at the beginning of the session:

As facilitator, my job is to help us get this job done today. You're not happy if we're not done. Your boss isn't happy and I'm not happy if we're not done. So, I see my job as being in charge of convergence and finishing.

I need your permission to push, push, push for convergence and closure. Of course, you have my permission to push back with, "Whoa, wait a minute, we're in the middle of a rich discussion. I know you want to move on, but this is really important, so we need to go a little deeper."

Then, for a short time, I will wait. Then I will push again. Somebody's got to do it, and I'm willing to be that person, but I need your permission. I'll keep us on track, and you'll get some great work done. Do I have your permission?

Because this can be a sensitive area, if you feel that the group is going to be resistant to your attempts to keep herding it, it may be wise to have somebody from outside your work group (an external consultant or internal change manager) facilitate the meeting.

In Summary

The next time you hear a bloated Blah-blah Blob rolling into a meeting:

➢ Have the group stand
➢ Break large groups into smaller groups
➢ Use Carousel Brainstorming for rich idea generation
➢ Use Dot Technology to read the room
➢ Employ the Can You Live With It consensus model
➢ Push to closure

The Second "Drag on" Collaboration: Unspeakable Ugly

"Trying to work with someone with whom you have unresolved baggage is like trying to ride a bike with an elephant on the handlebars."

-Dr. Marc Lewis

Observable Symptoms:

- Individuals act out dysfunctional, habitual behaviors, either out of frustration, stress, boredom or fear—any of which derails the group process.

- Unresolved old issues keep groups from truly collaborating and trusting one another and/or the manager.

- Something unsaid is deeply felt, making people clearly uncomfortable and unwilling to participate fully.

- The whole group is unable to confront and process issues productively.

Too Ugly for Words

Much is whispered at the coffee machine, but never talked about directly to the persons concerned. "Can you believe the nerve of that guy?" "I don't trust her as far as I can throw her!" "He is so annoying, I don't want him in any meeting!"

The result: When you are in a meeting with that person, there is an invisible but very ticked off dragon between you, inhibiting trust and good communication.

As long as no one really talks about the unspeakable issue, it stays big and strong and scary. If a rare individual appropriately confronts the person or situation and brings the issue to light, the "Unspeakable Ugly" can be dissipated. Yet most people try to ignore the Uglies and hope they go away. Of course, they rarely do. Mostly Uglies just sit around festering, sapping the vitality out of the team.

Here is a tip: separate the Unspeakable Uglies into two categories: those little annoying issues that reflect differences of style (the little Uglies), and the

> **Most people try to ignore the Uglies and hope they go away. Of course, they rarely do.**

problems of a deeper, more systemic nature (the big Uglies).

Dispensing With the LITTLE Unspeakable Uglies

We were working with a major semi-conductor company that had called us in for an intensive session to help merge three very different departments. The new, hybrid department was given one week to define roles. There were big-time turf issues with some very high-powered people, so the company needed to get this right.

After some preliminary interviews it was apparent that differences in personalities and communication styles could easily sabotage this delicate merger. For instance, there were a few hurt puppy types who withdrew and pouted when they didn't get their way. There was a steamroller bully type who wasted everyone's time with long stories. Most everyone was defending old turf. Our first task as facilitators was to get them to start working together. *(More on this merged team later.)*

Often, it's the little issues that can sabotage a team, *i.e.,* "He always interrupts"or "I can't *take* her long boring stories." At times, with these less intense issues, we've found that using *the right kind* of humorous self-disclosure works wonders.

Try the following two techniques to get the group to surface the little stylistic issues that create blocks: the "Invaders Checklist" and the "Help/Hinder Chart." Although these can be used at any time in a group's process, they are particularly effective when the group is just starting out, will be working together for a while and has identified "personality" issues. They will help the individuals take responsibility for their behavior in the group and help the entire group to be more responsible in overall communication.

Dragon Slayer #7: The Invaders Checklist

Introduce this exercise with humor and lightness. Remind the team that we all play roles in our lives, and in different settings. Place a flipchart with the list of "Invaders" in the front of the room. (See the chart on the next page.) Then go through the list, asking people to think about what roles they typically play out in a group setting.

Avoiding "The Invaders"

THE STORYTELLER
Prone to go off on a tangent with an interesting tale.

THE WALLFLOWER
Lets others do all the talking; doesn't participate.

THE INTERRUPTER
Cuts people off; leaves no space for others to respond.

THE SIDE TALKER
"How about those Giants!"

THE RAMBLER
Like the storyteller only not as interesting.

THE REPEATER
Likes to hear himself talk.

THE COWARDLY LION
Only offers safe ideas; takes no risks.

THE GENERALISSIMO
Takes over, becomes the boss.

THE WITHDRAWER
Pulls away. Thinks about something else.

THE HURT PUPPY
Wants her own way: "You didn't accept my idea so I'm not playing."

- Working in small groups of four to six people, each person describes which invader(s) sometimes "takes over his body."

- Within the group, have the team members ask what they can say to bring each other back to their productive selves. Encourage humor. For instance, the Generalissimo might suggests that others say, "Hey, the General is back," or, to a storyteller, "Hey, Lucy, we already heard that story."

- Have each person then write the name of their "Invader" in block letters on a small square card and slip it in or clip/tape it to their name tag or pocket. Underneath in lowercase lettering and in quotes, have them write what the group is to say or do to bring them back.

OR

- Have someone in each group write the team members' names on a flip chart, their particular brands of invader(s), and what the group can say to bring them back to their best group selves. Then have the scribes share their flip charts with the whole group. Post the lists on the wall during the meeting. Be a leader by humorously and positively using the list to stop unhelpful behavior.

A final note: It is important to be vigilant to keep things positive and safe. The reason this works so well is that individuals get to identify their own foibles. You don't want this process to digress into *others* identifying the personality challenge (which is not recognized by that person himself). If this happens, participants are likely to feel attacked, and, instead of building trust, trust is lessened.

Dragon Slayer #8: Help/Hinder Chart

This is similar to Dragon Slayer #7, but is less focused on personality quirks and more on general behaviors. It encourages candor, humor and teamwork.

Divide into small groups, then have each person tell what she often does to *help* group process, what she sometimes does to *hinder*, and what the team members can say when she drifts into hinder mode.

I model what I hope the group members might say with my own example: "What I do to help the group process is bring a lot of enthusiasm and expertise to this project. Plus, I value humor and like to use it when things get tense, to loosen things up. What I do to hinder is that I can get impatient and pushy sometimes when we really need to take more time to talk things out. When I do that, it would be a good idea to say, 'Be the Buddha, Ben.'"

Encourage the group to be casual, positive and to use humor. For instance, if someone is prone to get tense and anxious in meetings, invite the group to say, "Hey, Harry, chill

> "Search others for their virtues, thyself for thy vices."
>
> -Benjamin Franklin

out and breathe, brother. We need you back here at your most dazzling self!"

The scribe at a flip chart records "help" and "hinder" responses in a grid, which can then be posted on a wall.

The beauty of this exercise is that it creates a positive, open atmosphere of candor in the room, without much tension.

And Back at the Ranch. . .
So how did we resolve these "little issues" at that semi-conductor company that was merging divisions? The participants agreed ahead of time that when disruptive behavior created tension and discord, they would call one another on it, using the Invader's Checklist.

Yes, some people still dug in their heels at first. However, they soon saw that this new communication approach allowed them to be systematic enough to move forward instead of feeling negative and staying stuck. It got the group going in a humorous and positive direction that became the model for the whole integration process.

The BIG Unspeakable Uglies

Sometimes it ain't just the little issues. Sometimes life throws you a hardball. And something big and ugly is sitting center stage — though everyone acts like it doesn't exist. Think about your work. Haven't you seen a situation where key members of the group are locked in an unspoken power struggle that is throwing the whole game off? Maybe a major downsizing has happened and nobody is talking about it. Maybe a re-org was poorly communicated and people are feeling unfairly treated. Scratch the surface and you will find that the team lacks trust.

Scratch a little deeper and you will often find that this mistrust stems from some recent conflict with the company, the team or between specific people. Even trickier, the problem could lie with the manager. Because dealing with a Big Ugly dragon is uncomfortable, people will wish to avoid the whole area. However, if you proceed with an important meeting or a planning session *without addressing* with these morale killers, you won't have a chance.

When dealing with these kinds of issues, it is critical that you have the support of the manager. To garner this support, meet with him or her before the session, and explain how you will be addressing the Ugly, as well as what the positive outcomes for both the manager and group will be. If this person is "on your side," the group will have a greater sense of safety as it confronts the issues.

Do you always need to dig out the Uglies? NO.

If the group is only going to be working together for a short time, and the meeting is not of a critical nature, it is usually more efficient to just invest time and energy in the task at hand.

Also, if the issues are particularly thorny, or you are not comfortable with the expression of emotion, you should not try to run the conflict resolution session yourself. Your company probably has trained people on staff who know how to run these sensitive sessions. If not, get an outside facilitator with proven experience.

When I was green I did NOT take my own advice. While working with an entrenched culture with many 30-year veterans on the job, I sensed that something unsaid was holding up the group process. Clearly, some old personal business was festering underneath the surface.

After some digging, I uncovered an endless war that had been raging between the accounting and manufacturing departments, both headed by strong personalities. I couldn't figure the depth of this animosity. Yet it was a real problem and was spilling into every facet of the departments. Because I was too green to know when *not to go there,* I pressed on. When I got the two department heads to confront the issue head on, one yelled at the other, "I'll never forgive you for sleeping with my wife!" It wasn't pretty and it didn't help.

> If the baggage is old and heavy, trust issues must first be unloaded. Blithely press on and the session will just be some *game for the day.*

On the other hand, if the baggage is old and heavy, or the decisions on the table require complete alignment, you must first unload that baggage and deal with the trust issues. Blithely press on and the work will just be some "game for the day" with no follow through. If the problems and dysfunction are deep and long-standing (particularly if they involve the manager or team leader), then a separate conflict resolution session should be held prior to the planning session.

So, have the finesse to know when to push, when not to push, and when to turn a problem over to a conflict resolution manager. However, if the problems are the normal kind that plague work teams, if the boss is cooperative and open, if the group will be meeting on an ongoing basis, and if you feel comfortable doing it, here are a few alternate pain relievers for the Big Uglies.

Dragon Slayer #9: Mirror, Mirror

This is a relatively anonymous and quick intervention. As mentioned before, you need the approval and cooperation of the manager or team leader to proceed without resistance. Before the meeting begins, tape flip charts up around the room with something like the following questions on them:

- How are we an effective team?

- Where does the team fall short and why?

- What's great about this organization?

- What has really hurt you or ticked you off over the past year?

- Is it still worth trying to take this organization to the next level? Why or why not?

Using wide felt-tipped pens and Post-it notes, have everyone roam around the room at their own pace, putting up Post-it note responses to each of questions on the wall. Ask people to first read what Post-it responses are already up on the chart and check the ones they agree with and then write their own Post-it responses.

When everyone is finished giving input, have volunteers at each flip chart cluster the Post-its and report the general results, one chart at a time. The discussion that follows each report is usually rich and powerful.

Dragon Slayer #10: Prerequisites for Greatness Inventory

This technique is a great way to focus the group on some important elements of success, preparing them to challenge ineffective, habitual group behavior. Before this exercise, speak with the manager, and as many of the participants as possible, to be sure you understand the team dynamics. Before starting an initiative, project or planning session, introduce the activity, perhaps saying something like the following:

Before we get started making decisions about future directions for this group, we need to take a hard look at ourselves as a team. Is this group really capable of the kind of great collaboration that will lead to making real changes? To make certain that we are fully ready to move forward together, let's take stock of where we are as a team.

Next, introduce six "prerequisites for greatness." As you do, explain that these characteristics must be strongly present if the team is going to reinvent itself and reach a new level of effectiveness.

These areas are:

1. **Trust**
   Look around the room. Can you depend on the people in this group? Do you think we have a foundation to work together – or is credibility shot? Do you feel safe with these people?

2. **Passion**
   Does this group have the passion and energy to sustain this project/initiative?

3. **Honesty**
   Look around the room again. Can we be candid with each other?

4. Manager and Team in Sync

Here's a toughie: Are the team and the manager in sync about vision, mission, values and goals? If not, the output will be lackluster and fear-driven.

5. No Limiting Assumptions

Can we really keep an open mind, or will our negative attitudes bring us down?

6. No Old Baggage

Do we carry old hurts, wounds and memories that keep team members in old blaming, resistant ways?

To increase the level of candor, break the large group into small groups of four to six people. Then ask them to rate the whole team for these six areas, giving a score of 0 to 100 per cent.

Ask them to be prepared to explain the reason for their responses, high or low. Then record each team's answer on a grid on a flip chart at the front of the room. *The scores are not that important.* The real power of this exercise is in the discussion that follows. It gets the team to talk about these issues in a deep, but fairly non-threatening way.

This amazing process in itself is usually enough to clear the air and help the group prepare for a very powerful planning event. Again, more significant interventions like conflict resolution may be necessary if the team problems are deep. After the air is cleared, you might want to say something like:

Okay, so it seems like this team has been dealt a lot of 2's and 3's along with some kings and aces. Now, the question is, "Do you still want to work together for the next two [or one or whatever] days to build a future together?"

Then go around and ask each person, "Are you 'in'?" (They always are, but the ritual of going around the room is powerful).

Just making the invisible visible has great power. Once old issues have been aired, a gust of new energy is freed up to do powerful planning.

Dragon Slayer #11: The Innocent Messenger

This technique is a good one to use when the situation is potentially more threatening, when resistance is stronger or when discomfort with management has been identified. It is imperative that the manager or leader of the group fully buys into the process—because that person will almost certainly be uncomfortable while it is happening, and needs to have been well prepared.

Before you do this exercise meet with the manager or leader to prep for what could come up. Alert her that she might feel an unsettling challenge to her authority. Explain that people need to vent, fairly or unfairly. Also, explain that she as the leader could likely become a lightning rod for frustration if this venting is not allowed.

Here is the good news: if the manager or leader is up to the challenge, there will be serious benefits in store for her. She will have a career-altering chance to demonstrate her leadership by simply listening, not getting defensive, not denying, not arguing or interrupting. If she can take criticism well, create trust and even say "thank you" at the end, her stock will rise in people's estimation.

To start the process, divide the group into small groups of four to six. Give each group questions to answer. They could be the six questions from "Mirror, Mirror." (How are we an effective team? Where does the team fall short and why? What's great about this organization? What really hurt you or ticked you off over the past year? Is it still worth trying to take this organization to the next level?)

Additionally or alternatively, if you suspect that there are issues with the leader and his/her management style, then you will also want to add something like the following:

- What do you like about the way _____ manages?

- What don't you particularly like about the way _____ manages?

- What other suggestions do you have for _____ to help him manage even better?

Then have each group choose an "innocent messenger." The messenger's job will be to report the findings to the group at large. Ask everyone to be finished in 15-20 minutes.

While the groups are working, the facilitator takes the manager/leader of the group out into the hallway or to another room, where he answers the same questions.

When everyone is finished, bring all the messengers and the leader into the center of the room, seated in chairs in a circle. Everyone else should be seated around this inner circle. Have the manager encourage candor from the messengers and guarantee that there will be no retribution (that is, the messenger will not be "shot"!).

In turn, the messengers should all state that none of the things they are about to say came from them. Rather they all came from others in their group. (Even though this is untrue, it gets a big laugh and eases the tension.)

> **The biggest obstacle to learning anything is believing that you already know it.**
>
> - Karl Albrecht

Then, for each question, call on each innocent messenger to give the group's responses and reasons. (Get all of the group's responses to the first question before going on to the next question.)

Once you have all responses to a given question, let anyone else from outside the inner circle address the topic, if they choose. Finally, when the discussion is complete for question #1, ask the leader if he'd like to make a short statement about what he heard, before going on the next question. Give him this option after each question is completely discussed.

Although the questions themselves might be the same as the ones written on the Dragon Slayer #8 wall charts, the answers will be received far more powerfully. Speaking one's mind directly to the manager has far more impact on the group, both in terms of strength of expression and in building trust within the group.

Dragon Slayer #12: Neutralizing Disrupters

As any good manager knows, conflict and disagreement in and of themselves are not bad. They only become disruptive for the group when some people create conflict just to get attention or express displaced frustration or irritation.

We had this same situation at, of all places, a yoga retreat center where one expects, well. . .enlightened interaction. Yet in this organization, the director would call staff meetings, then get so mad he'd hijack the agenda and rant, or worse, he'd start yelling at everyone. What do you do with this kind of situation? Neutralize, neutralize.

So far in the Dragon Slayers for the Unspeakable Ugly, we have suggested techniques in which the group manages difficult situations. However, with this Dragon Slayer, we will be introducing an approach for you, the leader or facilitator of the group, to deal with difficult *individuals*. This strategy works along a continuum, with the less confrontational and more win/win techniques being introduced before the more confrontational. We strongly recommend that you try the earlier ones before the later ones.

Avoid the Situation

Avoiding the situation is always the easiest approach for all concerned, though it does take some time. Surface issues proactively through pre-meeting interviews in which you ask participants to frankly tell you what the challenges are in the group. Plan the structure of the meeting using this information and include techniques that avoid confrontational situations, such as dots, carousel brainstorming, *etc.*

By using some of the techniques introduced throughout this book, you will greatly minimize the chance of bad apples ruining the applesauce. As previously stated, the large group should be a place for the small teams to make presentations or very brief comments. However, there will always be some people ready to jump in anywhere and drive everybody nuts.

Respond Neutrally

So let's say that you've set up a good structure, but someone seems to be intent on making his or her agenda the focus of the meeting. Be brief and neutral: acknowledge the disrupter, recognize their resistance and move on. Then address questions to the larger group, while occasionally doubling back to check in with the disrupter. Give the disrupter plenty of attention, yet keep the response fairly low-key.

Remember that when someone stops the flow with a comment, he may simply be airing a legitimate point. On the other hand, he could just enjoy messing up processes and slowing things down. He could just like hearing himself talk. Here's an example of how to quickly get past the issue and move on.

Lets assume a small breakout team has just made a presentation for a certain course of action or wording of a statement. Then someone raises a concern. For instance, this person we'll call Charlie says, "I think that on the second statement up there, the word 'greater' should really read 'better'." Instead of responding to Charlie, the wise leader should ADDRESS THE WHOLE GROUP with something like:

"Thank you Charlie. Okay, who agrees with Charlie?" (It could go either way. If no one or almost no one raises a hand, then say), "Charlie, your point is good, yet nobody (or very few) agree with you. Can you live with it the way it is?" Most often, Charlie can live with it, and he is satisfied that he has been heard. So, you are finished and ready to move on.

If a lot of people raise their hands when you ask about Charlie's point, then make this a group decision: "Can you live with it if we changed 'greater' to 'better'?" Usually, the group will give their okay and you're finished and can move on. Yet once in a while, even with reasonable people, you will have to quickly wordsmith a compromise. (Keep a Post-it pad and pen nearby when facilitating this kind of interchange.)

Hyper Focus

What if someone won't drop it? By this point in the process, your disrupter will have become totally frustrated because the Post-it notes thing has kept him from his usual negative speeches. But now he senses his chance. He sees an opening. So, let's say "Bob" raises his hand and you ask for his issue and Bob says it.

Then you ask the other group members if it is a concern for them. Nobody raises a hand and you ask Bob if he can live with it the way it is. If he says vehemently, "No, I can't live with it," then what what do you do?

> **What if you ask Bob if he can "live with it" and he vehemently says, "No, I can't live with it!" Then what do you do?**

Answer: You hyper-focus on the disrupter. Keep coming up with alternative options and asking if he can live with them. You say, "Okay, Bob, what *would* work for you? What if I changed this? Would that work for you? No, okay, let's see, how about this?" Eventually, the rest of the group will get tired and irritated with Bob (who probably always does this kind of thing).

They'll start saying things like, "Come on, Bob, let's move on," and eventually Bob is going to say, "Okay, okay, go on." To which you'll say, "Are you sure? Are you sure you don't want to discuss this further? I want to make certain you can live with it, Bob." And *hallelujah*, he'll finally say, "Yes, go on."

The atmosphere of respect has been preserved, and Bob will be much less likely to continue to disrupt the group.

Take a Break

Sometimes people get so heated that it is wiser to allow time for emotions to settle down, and let the saner part resurface. So take ten, and when you come back, restate the problem in neutral terms that focus on issues and not personalities.

Respond Offline

When the behavior persists, it can be effective to meet with the person offline, either during a break or between sessions. Outline the behavior that you are concerned about, and negotiate agreement on what will work to meet the individual's and group's needs.

Confront the Person

Confront this person in the group with their behavior and the effects of that behavior, only after trying everything else and only if you feel you are competent in dealing with strong emotions, including your own.

Back at the Yoga Center. . .

The Unspeakable Uglies problem with the yoga retreat leader was so severe we had to use literally every dragon slaying technique. We employed responding neutrally, hyper-focusing on the leader, taking a break, responding offline and eventually confronting him.

If you cringe thinking about trying it with your own pain-in-the-neck group member, know this: it worked. The leader "got it." No one was fired—not even me, the facilitator. After this very powerful training, the quiet little yoga retreat center in the woods had productive—even peaceful—staff meetings again. Ommmm.

In Summary

The next time you see the Unspeakable Ugly lurking around a meeting:

- ➤ Make an Invaders Checklist
- ➤ Employ the Help/Hinder Charts
- ➤ Take a Prerequisites for Greatness Inventory
- ➤ Think Mirror, Mirror, and use a team analysis
- ➤ Confront the Manager through Innocent Messengers
- ➤ Neutralize the Disrupters

Chapter 2: The Magic Cauldron of Innovation: Igniting the Spark

"The real voyage of discovery is not in seeing new landscapes, but in having new eyes."

-Marcel Proust

> In this chapter we are going to stir things up in the Cauldron of Innovation, and find new ways to ignite the spark that is waiting in your team.

In my Ph.D. work at Washington University in St. Louis, I studied under professor Richard DeCharms. He had been a student of David McClelland's at Harvard University, a world-renowned social psychologist who studied human motivation.

Dr. DeCharms developed the "Origin-Pawn" theory. He hypothesized, and later demonstrated, that if a child is unconsciously treated as a "pawn" by well-meaning parents and teachers, that child will grow up to be a well-behaved, responsible, unimaginative, uncreative follower. On the other hand, if she is treated as an "origin" of her own behavior and choices, the child will develop into an independent, self-initiating, creative leader.

DeCharms' major work was in schools with teachers and students. But if he had made the same type of non-participant observations in today's corporations, he would clearly have discovered the same origin/pawn behavioral results.

Every leader I know pays lip service to innovation. They all say that we have to have new ideas, that we must "get out of the box," take risks, be open to alternative ideas, learn from mistakes.

Yet those same leaders unintentionally construct an atmosphere that stifles innovation and encourages people to be risk-adverse, politically astute pawns.

In some organizations, people prize politeness. They go to great extremes to avoid mistakes and conflict. They are usually firefighter types, who stay tactical and focused on the short-term. Attached to following established processes, they have learned to be highly political. These kinds of cultures are rarely the ones that innovate.

Organizations where people are first and foremost creative, funny and put no premium on being polite, are far more likely to be innovative. At these firms, the atmosphere is vibrant. Mistakes are made and forgiven. Action, not perfection, is reinforced.

The staff is jazzed about their mission, not just a paycheck. In these innovative, collaborative shops, employees tend to be long-term thinkers who are motivated by values. The leaders model the same risk-taking and out-of-the-box thinking that they seek in employees.

So what has happened to the magic Cauldron of Innovation that the Genie believes in? What keeps teams from innovation? Often two dragons are busy stalking the troops, the "Political Chicken" and the "Idea Eater." Let's examine how they show up and what to do about them.

The First "Drag on" Innovation: Political Chicken

*"If you always do what you always did,
you'll always get what you always got."*

-Anonymous

Observable Symptoms:

- When faced with the need to generate new ideas, people are stuck in their old ruts, and trot out the same worn-out suggestions.

- Group members exhibit a lack of risk-taking and creativity in problem solving.

If your team is like most, whenever there is a problem to be solved, people do the same thing: call a meeting. Everybody comes into the conference room, sits around the table, and somebody at a blank flip chart says, "Okay people, come on, think! What's the solution? Who has an idea?" Often, everyone just looks at one another blankly or repeats old worn-out excuses or complaints. Sometimes a few ideas are offered, but they are often things like, "Let's form a task force," or "Let's do a survey." CLUNK.

Three Dragon Slayers To Chase Out "Political Chickens"

Here are some ideas for chasing out those Political Chickens. First, forget those demoralizing meetings for a moment. When do your best ideas come? If you are like most people of whom I've asked this question, your best ideas pop out when you are either moving around or reflecting.

Over and over respondents have told me "When I'm driving," "While jogging," "I'm cycling," "I'm cutting my lawn," "I'm walking," "I'm pacing," "My best ideas come when I'm moving!"

The rest of the responses involve reflection, such as, "I'm just going to sleep," "I'm just waking up," "I'm in the shower," "In my sleep," "Mostly when I'm in downtime!"

Clearly, most of us get our best ideas when moving or reflecting. Yet how do most organizations brainstorm? Aren't people usually sitting, interminably cooped up with each other with no reflection time?

Dragon Slayer #13: Reflection

If there is a lost art in the Western world, surely it is reflection. We pejoratively call it downtime. Heaven forbid we should have anyone sitting, thinking and seemingly doing nothing for very long.

Consider the brilliant mathematician, Rene Descartes, who lived in the 17th century. Rene, born into a wealthy family, was sent to the best schools and became an incredible scholar.

Yet Rene was bored stiff.

So his parents suggested law school, but that didn't work. After law school, he did a stint in the military, but that didn't take either. Frustrated, Rene said, "I quit, I'm not doing anything more!" His parents said, "You can't quit, you're too brilliant. You can't waste your mind." "Nope," said the young man, "I quit. I am going to do nothing." For two years, Rene Descartes became the 17th century version of the couch potato. He laid around. He slept. (This being the south of France, he ate incredibly well and took long picturesque strolls with beautiful French women. . .but I digress.) Not understanding the wisdom of reflection, his loved ones wrung their hands, "Oh, poor Rene, what a waste of a great mind. What a tragedy!"

Then one night, after two years, in the middle of a dream, the idea for the scientific method came to Rene Descartes. The scientific method is the accepted worldwide basis for how all knowledge is verified — in short, how we know what we know.

OK, it's true that the idea for the scientific method didn't come from a guy bussing tables. Yes, this man had the knowledge and background needed to conceive of it. But what's often overlooked or downgraded is the space and time it took for his ideas to incubate and develop. We also need to build incubation time into our idea-generation.

*   *   *

Here's another example. About 25 years ago, the Japanese were streaking past the United States with innovations. They were churning out new ideas and fresh, successful products. The U.S. wasn't doing nearly as well. Even though it was the smaller country with fewer resources, and had to fight its way back from WWII bombings, Japan surpassed us in creative thinking.

So, the United States sent a contingent of sociologists and anthropologists to Japan to find out just what it was that enabled the Japanese to be so innovative. There was one spectacular finding that the U.S. did not anticipate: in traditional Japanese culture it is considered rude to walk up to somebody who is sitting, staring out the window and seemingly doing nothing. It is a grave breach of etiquette to interrupt them. Yet, if they're working on a machine or clearly on a task it's fine to interrupt them.

Funny, in North America it's the opposite. If a person is working on a machine we say, "Oh, he's being productive, better not bother him." Yet if the same guy is staring out the window we say, "Oh, he's not busy." So, we have no trouble going up and interrupting his thoughts. "You're not busy are you?" "No, I was just thinking up the Scientific Method, no problem!"

* * *

One last anecdote: When I turned 40, I had the proverbial mid-life crisis. I got divorced and sold my successful business, an advertising agency that had made me lots of money but had given me little fulfillment. I was confused and didn't see what was next. I had done everything people said would make me a success. Tenacious, opportunistic, I never stopped. Respected by many, I was neither fulfilled nor happy—just busy.

I did all the hackneyed things people do when they have a mid-life crisis. No, I didn't get a new, red sports car or a sexy girlfriend half my age. I did the spiritual mid-life crisis thing; I went to Santa Fe and then later to India to "find the meaning of life."

Unfortunately, no ancient Indian guru slipped out of the shadows at a street bazaar and whispered enlightenment; however, I did get the answer I was seeking. Early one morning, about 5 a.m., I was sitting looking out over the Indian Ocean in an enchanting city called Goa. I was musing about my life, and thinking about the ocean.

"Clearly, the ocean is one of the most powerful things in nature," I thought. As the frothy waves cut into the rocks, I looked at the shoreline and realized how insignificant mere rock was against the unstoppable force of the ocean. Then it hit me like a whack upside the head: the power of the ocean does not come from just flowing. The power of the ocean comes from its flowing and then ebbing, and then flowing and ebbing again.

At that moment, I realized that what I really needed in my life was, well…ebb training. I know it sounds funny. I, like many other other driven people, had never learned to ebb.

> "I've re-dedicated myself to learn how to ebb…not just flow."

When I was young I was told to flow. When anything went wrong, people around me would say, "Just try harder! Work more! Flow, flow!"

But now I had a new thought: ebb. Eureka! Instead of pushing, let things go. Breathe deeply, try on a different speed for a little while.

Buoyed, I re-dedicated myself to learning how to ebb. I found that it's trickier than it looks. My typical American male instinct was to do more flowing. So I frequented a yoga ashram. . .and pretty soon sought to be its marketing director. *OK, OK, it took awhile to understand this ebb thing.*

Our whole society needs ebb training. There is great power in reflection for it is in times of reflection that ideas come.

What does reflection look like? It can be as simple as having your meeting participants go for a short walk and think for a few moments about what has been happening. Or, you can do it more formally, by handing out a notebook with a section just for writing reflections, having small groups discuss how they feel a session has gone, or having the large group generate reflections about an activity.

Listen up, leaders and facilitators. When you lead brainstorming and decision-making sessions, give the participants at least 5-10 minutes in the middle of the session to just be by themselves and reflect on all that has been discussed. Let the knowledge they bring in, the experiences of the day, and the problem at hand, sink in. Then witness the amazing results.

Dragon Slayer #14: The Fab Four Brainstorming Styles

The word "creative" has been distorted over the past decade. You hear people say, "Oh, I'm not creative, I can't come up with really original ideas," or "I'm not creative, I can't get-out-of-the-box," or "I'm not creative, I've never been very clever!" Well, if you think about the base word "create," it takes a lot more than generating a lot of clever ideas to truly create something. Who is the real "creator" of a building? Is it the developer who had the vision? Is it the architect who designed it or the contractor who oversaw the project? Maybe it's the bricklayer who actually laid the foundation? Well, of course, it is all of them!

There are different kinds of brainstormers. The "creative thinking" craze of the last twenty years suggests that the "best" brainstormer is one who comes up with as many ideas as possible without judgment, without criticism. Certainly there is a place for this kind of idea generation. However, a team of people who are fantastic at coming up with a lot clever ideas quickly, but don't have some of the more practical perspectives and abilities, will have a lot of nothing at the end of the day. No creation.

I have observed over the years four kinds of creative brainstorming styles: Visionaries, Generators, Integrators and Pragmatists.

- Visionaries: Big (10,000 foot) view, broad-thinkers, visual, strategic
- Generators: Spontaneous, prolific, unbounded
- Integrators: Holistic, balancing, mediators
- Pragmatists: Analytical, practical, tactical

I have noticed that the best brainstorming teams are ones that include all of these types. When creating brainstorming teams, to the extent possible, try to include a mix of individuals that have all of these styles.

Most people can identify which kind of creative brainstormer they are. Ask them! You will see a big difference in the results when all parts of the creative process are addressed and each person knows they have an important, key role in their group. You'll see them proudly working at a high level of effectiveness. Once you do it this way, you will never again arbitrarily put brainstorming teams together.

Dragon Slayer #15: Rapid Fire Brainstorming

One of the ways to ignite the spark in your group is to use the fun and stimulating "Rapid Fire Brainstorming" technique when you need to generate ideas. When your team is on the hunt for breakthrough ideas, build in a special mini-session where you speed up the whole process to a breakneck pace. Brainstorming accesses that magical place where either the Genie or the Dragons could enter. If you go slowly, it becomes too easy to filter, to doubt and to hesitate. Go fast and there is less time for the internal critic dragon to bluster his way in.

Need an example? A global credit card company based in New York wanted a cross-departmental team to come up with some good ideas—and fast. Specifically, the senior leadership team wanted to attract the affluent segment of cardholders who pay off their balances every month. Their time frame: six hours.

At first the skeptics, who said it was ridiculous, ruled the day. "It's naïve to think we can come up with any viable ideas this quickly," they groused, "or even get to the right questions to ask!"

But the naysayers eventually lost to the Rapid Fire Brainstormers. In just six hours, they not only came up with the right questions, they crafted really good ideas. By the end of the seminar, the group had brainstormed several excellent ideas to take to the bosses. I don't know who was more amazed, the Rapid Fire Brainstormers or their impressed senior leadership team!

As we did with this global credit card company, encourage your group to brainstorm quickly, even recklessly—at least at first. You can always tone things down. Toning things *up* is the challenge. So set a fast pace, and keep it short, too—go on too long and the same tired ideas will start being raised by a group of tired, grumpy people.

It will not take long for one good idea to pop out, if the conditions are right. To brainstorm any well-stated question, 30 minutes will usually be an optimal amount of time. Before starting, everyone should be fully briefed and knowledgeable.

Rapid Fire Brainstorming is a process that helps overcome the normal inertia and self-consciousness of the typical brainstorming process. Here's how it works:

Rapid Fire Brainstorming

- Stand: go fast, go wide!
- Cluster
- Go wide for each promising cluster
- Stop and cherry-pick
- *Option: If stuck, use a Creative Thinking Technique*
- Individual reflection
- Go deep with the promising ideas
- Prepare best idea(s) for presentation

Rapid Fire Brainstorming Instructions:

1. Stand: go fast, go wide!

In this technique, arm each person with a Post-it note pad and pen, and ask them to basically, well. . . think fast and write graffiti.

Have them stand and answer a question with the first thing that comes to mind, whether it makes any sense or not. If the question is, "How can we reduce the company's debt?" then participants quickly generate responses and put them up on Post-it notes on a flip chart.

For instance, they might answer with, "Let's sell the company to a big conglomerate with deep pockets" or "Let's get Bill Gates to buy us" or, "Stop spending money on useless seminars like this one!" Encourage them to put up whatever comes to mind.

Here is what you might say: *Have a good time and go fast. That's how great ideas are going to pop out! Don't just write your post-it notes, read what your teammates put up on the board. That may make you think of something else. Then write it up! Try to not make judgments. Just keep creating lots of ideas, and have lots of fun.*

Have the group "go wide" for about five minutes, then stop and review.

2. Stop and cluster

Ask the group to cluster the data into categories, by moving the Post-its into like-idea groups (also called "affinity groupings.") Once categorized or clustered, have them name each cluster.

3. Go wide for each promising cluster

Continue brainstorming each cluster as before, still "going wide." However, this time, direct the whole team's thoughts to a certain category of ideas. Pick the cluster that is most promising to the team and go with that until a plateau is reached, then go on to a different cluster. Remember, keep going wide— keep having fun and adding ideas. Don't worry about covering up the post-it notes from before. If they're worthwhile, someone will pull them out later. Do this for five minutes.

4. Stop and cherry-pick

Now ask the team members to stop and ask one another, "Okay, what have we got? Anything good?" If there are some potentially workable ideas, even if they aren't fleshed out yet, take those one or two Post-it notes off the flip chart, turn the flip chart page over, and put the one or two interesting/promising ideas on the top of the next blank flip chart page.

5. (Optional): Use a creative thinking technique

If you have not gotten a good idea at this juncture and the team is still stuck, use one of the creative thinking techniques found in Addendum A of this book (or use your own idea–generating process).

6. Individually reflect

This is the point where you ask team members to reach deep inside and reflect. Have them take a short walk outside, gaze out the window or lie down somewhere. Ask them to do whatever it takes to really be alone with their thoughts and let ideas gestate. After this reflection break, have everyone return to the brainstorming groups and share what new ideas have emerged. Take five minutes for this activity.

7. Go deep with the promising ideas

At this point, the team will have chosen one or two promising ideas. Now it will be time to put the meat on the bones and "go deep." Have everyone focus on developing these one or two rough ideas, individually or together. Instead of going wide, have them go deeper with these ideas and fill in the details. Then, have them write up the idea(s) that they think could work.

8. Prepare best idea(s) for presentation

Keep the idea presentation sheet super simple so all can grasp it. Your groups should use the following format, on one flip chart page, to present their ideas.

IDEA PRESENTATION

Idea Name:

Description:

Benefits:

Tell them to put the name of the idea, the description and the benefits on one piece of flip chart paper, reminding them that all they need is one idea. Remind them that a good name, often an acronym or word-play, helps sell an idea. Have them describe the idea and what it includes. Finally, have the group list the benefits.

A final note: As I said, earlier in this chapter, in Addendum A you will find two great brainstorming techniques which I learned from

Mitch Ditkoff of Idea Champions in Woodstock, N.Y. In my mind, Mitch is *the* master of creative thinking. If you want to go deeper in this area—call Mitch!

In Summary

If the Political Chicken comes home to roost:

➤ Build in time to reflect
➤ Use the Fab Four Brainstorming Styles
➤ Do Rapid Fire Brainstorming

The Second "Drag on" Innovation: Idea-Eater

"The man with a new idea is a crank until the idea succeeds."

-Mark Twain

Observable Symptoms:

- People are unwilling to break out of old patterns because of limiting assumptions.

- Staff has chronic negative reactions to new ideas.

Often team members act from assumptions and beliefs that are so ingrained that they don't even see them, or react in knee-jerk, negative ways. Either way, they miss out on the ideas and energy that are going to carry their organization forward.

Dragon Slayer #16: Move Past Limiting Assumptions

Unexamined beliefs are like seeing through colored glass, and sometimes we need to look at the glass for a moment. We need to examine how we limit our effectiveness when we inadvertently limit our sight.

Limiting assumptions about what is appropriate or possible reduces our options. We stay practical, small and unobtrusive, *which isn't a hot M.O. for breakthrough thinking.*

A limiting assumption can be deadly for organizations because it keeps the team from realizing its potential. Here are some astoundingly wrong limiting assumptions that were taken as givens in their time:

In the nineteenth century, Dr. Dionysus Lardner concluded: *"Rail travel at high speeds is not possible because passengers, unable to breath, would die of asphyxia."*

In 1899, Charles Duell, Commissioner of the U.S. Office of Patents, let the world know that: *"Everything that can be invented has been invented."*

At the turn of the 20th century, Thomas Edison insisted: *"The phonagraph has no commercial value."*

In 1903, Wilber Wright declared: *"Man will not fly for 50 years."*

In 1909, Scientific American magazine reported: *"Automobiles have clearly reached the limit of development as no improvement of a radical nature has been introduced over the past year."*

In the forties, movie pioneer Darryl F. Zanuck, scoffed: *"Video won't be able to hold on to any market. People will soon get tired of staring at a plywood box every night."*

In 1943, Thomas J. Watson, Chairman of the Board of IBM: *"I think there is a world market for about five computers."*

In 1957, the Editor of *Prentice Hall* magazine, let Americans know: *"I have spoken with the best business minds in this country and I assure you that data processing is a fad that won't last out the year."*

Business Week, 1968: *"With over 50 foreign cars already on sale here, the Japanese auto industry isn't likely to carve out a very big slice of the U.S. market."*

And, finally, in 1977, Ken Olsen, President of Digital Equipment Corporation boldly proclaimed: *"There is no reason for any individual to have a computer in their home."*

These leaders really believed these statements, all of which turned out to be patently untrue. *Help your team* by introducing the concept of limiting assumptions. One way to do this is to post these humorous limiting assumptions and challenge the group to think of ways that they are also limiting their thinking. Another is to generate a list of assumptions about the issue at hand, and pick out four or five to challenge and discuss.

This happened dramatically in a planning session I led for a big chemical company in Tennessee. As I often recommend, a large cross section of the exempt employees participated. A worker named Marilyn was the only woman and certainly the least senior person in the small brainstorming group. Our task was to wrestle with how to reduce skyrocketing rail costs due to lack a of competition in the area. By the way, Marilyn knew very little on this subject.

We brainstormed for a while, but no one came up with any useful ideas. Finally, Marilyn suggested The company use the rail line across the river. When the men rolled their eyes, explaining that there was no way to get the product across the river, Marilyn reminded them that there was a pipe. The men responded with more eye-rolling, "Yes, but this pipe is used to carry fresh water."

Undaunted, Marilyn suggested that it could be used to send the product over the river and then cleaned out. Again the men put up another roadblock, condescendingly explaining that the cleaning costs would be prohibitive.

Then Marilyn asked, "Would it cost more than the obscene amounts the rail company demands for their services?" The men coughed, moved restlessly in their seats and quietly said they did not know.

Marilyn's lack of limiting assumptions and fresh thinking prompted some participants to investigate cleaning out the pipe and using the competitive rail provider. When the existing provider got wind of this, it lowered its price by $1 million a year, saving Marilyn's company a bundle.

Way to go, Marilyn.

Dragon Slayer #17: Entertain The Fantastic!

When considering new ideas, it is important to be practical. However, there is danger in being too practical too soon. Being practical too soon eliminates fantasizing, and fantasizing is an important tool in breakthrough thinking and innovations. Entertaining the fantastic is crucial to moving past limiting assumptions, which in turn leads to generating new, innovative ideas.

When a lot of people are saying what they can't possibly do or accomplish, put it down on paper for all to see. Literally make a list on a flip chart, titled, "What we CAN'T possibly do." Then divide everyone into brainstorming groups of three or four people, and have them brainstorm how they *could* do those things that are "impossible." The creative results will astound them and open up their thinking.

Albert Einstein said that his ability to fantasize was more important than any knowledge he possessed. Gary Kasparov, the world champion chess player, repeatedly beat all the computers the world could throw in his path. These computers had been designed to play chess better than humans by incorporating the best moves, strategies and games of 12 of the world's greatest grand chess masters.

Yet for years, Gary Kasparov just kept beating the darn machines. Asked to explain how this was possible, he said, "Because a machine can't fantasize. I can."

Suspending the practical and entertaining the fantastic is critical to success. Don't you know colleagues who carry practical filters and slap them on everything throughout their day? If something is not practical then *that's it!* They give it no more thought. If these people were in charge of developing some of the world's great projects, you'd be reading this book by candlelight and I'd be writing with a typewriter.

Big surprise: Most technical and analytical business people are generally practical types. Scientists look at things with a very critical eye and aren't ones to be taken in by wild, hair-brained schemes. Yet by quickly shutting down out-of-the-normal ideas, we are removing a potentially powerful tool from our tool kit. There are good answers in the realm of fantasy—crazy, but good—for they may be the triggers to some great and practical ideas. In order to have a great brainstorming session, the trainer must give permission and even push people into the realm of fantasy.

Once you have the seeds of a great idea you can always dial it back down and make it practical.

For instance, let's say you are looking for ways to get executive support. Maybe you brainstorming a great fantasy to go up to the corporate headquarters and throw water balloons at the executive team to team to get their attention. It would really work — only you'd probably get fired in the process.

> The leader must give the team permission – and even push people – into the realm of fantasy. You can always dial it back down and make it practical.

Yet this brainstorming activity gets you thinking how to dramatically get management's attention without getting in trouble. One group I know printed up a series of different memo pads, each with a different message that appeared on four successive Monday mornings on the executive team's desks.

For a great technique to "entertain the fantastic" check out "Wish, Wild Wish, Fantasy" in Addendum A.

Dragon Slayer #18: Make New Neural Connections

Brains learn by habitual repetition.

When you learn to play tennis, the instructor tells you, "Hold the racket here and whenever you see the ball, take a step out and swing your racket back." At first, you have to think about it: ball—step, and racquet back, ball—step, and racquet back. Over time, the neuron in your brain that carries the word "ball" and the neuron that has an impulse to take a step and take the racket back actually get physically closer together. They actually bend toward each other and form what is called a neural net, and the synapse between them speeds up. Eventually it's just automatic: You see the ball, and, like magic, "step and swing" just seem to happen by themselves.

Here's another example from video games. There is a Nintendo game where the bad guy comes out and the player is supposed to decapitate him. *(I'll leave the editorial comments about these games for another time!)* So I watch my kids do it and it goes like this: bad guy—head off, bad guy—head off. I'm scratching my head and asking myself, "How do they do that? I can hardly see the bad guy and they already cut his head off!" Well, as you probably know, it's because they've played the game

2,147,000 times. So after the 146,000[th] time, they've gotten blurry-fast at it.

If one is trying to play Nintendo or learning to play tennis, the habitual thinking that the brain does is great. But if the goal is a new idea for improving the morale at a company, and every time someone says "morale," people say, "Let's do a survey" or "Let's form a task force," they are severely limiting the company's options.

Yet, what else can we do?

> "Learning requires great energy. UN-learning and RE-learning requires even more. We must access higher brain functions to unbind the old."
>
> - Harold Lasswell

First we have to access a different part of our brain. The really bold, new answers reside where we least expect them. That's what innovative, creative thinking truly is. We have to search all around our brain and get out of that stuck neural net.

The good news is that this doesn't mean starting from scratch. Most great innovations are not totally new.

Instead, they are the connection between ideas that already existed. For instance, when I was growing up, every summer all the kids roller-skated. We clipped these ball-bearing things on our shoes and those were our skates. Then, in the winter, everybody ice-skated. Roller skating, ice-skating — they were two different things. Then somebody put them together and made roller-blading.

Consider another example of two familiar things recombined. Once music and television were very separate media categories. Then in the 1980s somebody put them together and made MTV, which is now a multi-billion dollar part of mainstream culture.

Answers to many problems already exist. The trick is putting previously unrelated thoughts or principles together. A hundred years ago, Heubline Company obtained the marketing and distribution rights to a new liquor from Russia called "vodka."

Unfortunately, when they tried to promote and sell this vodka, nobody bought the stuff. All their market research resulted in negative responses: "Vodka is not liquor. Liquor is colored brown, not clear. Liquor has an odor to it and this vodka is colorless and odorless." It appeared that the Heubline Company had bought the rights to *a dog*.

Then some Heubline exec got the brilliant idea to mix vodka with tomato juice or orange juice.

Today, vodka is the number-one liquor sold in this country and in the world. Nobody had to reinvent anything. They just had to put existing things together in a new way. These new connections in our brains come to us accidentally, when we're not trying. We're thinking about one thing and something triggers another thought and, all of a sudden, the idea is there: boom!

Once there was only the mimeograph, before Xerox invented the copier. Once we did math by longhand ledger, before Texas Instruments gave us the calculator. We used to all pay by cash before Mastercard *et al* invented credit cards. Some people were sitting around a room just like we do all the time. Can't we do what they did? Why not us?

To make new neural connections, invite your group to play with the idea, combining and recombining familiar ideas with the unfamiliar. For a great technique to do this, see the New Neural Connections Technique in Addendum A.

Dragon Slayer #19: LCS

What if your group generates some innovative ideas but that overly critical Idea Eater dragon returns? The genie is squashed and the idea dies a quick death. How can you keep people open and willing to share their ideas?

What generally happens when somebody comes up with a new idea? What do you hear? "We can't do it. It won't work in this culture. It's not in the budget. We tried that already, that will never fly — they'll never go for it, *etc.*" This naysaying is not because people are mean or not smart. It's just that analytical beings get focused on what's wrong and what's missing. They think they're being helpful by pointing out, "Gee, don't waste your time."

This deadly approach can poison the well. If every idea is met with why it won't work, a sea of negativity forms. We get deluded into falsely presuming that finding flaws is some big, important accomplishment, when in fact it is a no-brainer. In fact, at first, most ideas *are* quite flawed!

We all find fault, in fact, we *like* to find fault, especially with new ideas — but it is counter-productive. A new idea is like a baby bird in the wild. It's not pretty. It has a hairless body and is always stretching out its ugly scrawny neck for worms. Isn't that the way most ideas emerge: odd-looking and fragile? Like baby birds, new ideas are very easy to kill off.

Yet if you nurture a baby bird, if you bring it along, it can be beautiful and take off someday. Likewise, we must treat new ideas gingerly, like baby birds. They might start out ugly, they may not look like they'll fly, but they may someday soar.

So what do we do to reverse this natural inclination to kill ideas in their infancy? Try LCS, a unique group communication technique designed to protect new ideas and the people who come up with them.

LCS

LIKES:
First acknowledge what you like about the idea.
(If possible, come up with three things).

CONCERNS:
Second, express your concerns about the idea.

SUGGESTIONS:
Only then, make a suggestion for each concern: to either deal with each concern or make the idea better.

LCS powerfully counters our natural instinct to say no, shut down, and reject new ideas.

This approach reverses the harmful confidence-deflating order of how we often give feedback. Rather than starting with what naturally comes up first, that is, your concern ("It's not in the budget," "We tried that already," and so forth), start with what you like about the idea.

You might say, "Here is what I like about your idea, it creates a win-win," or "I agree that the budget has to be finished soon." You may have to stretch. "Gee, it's creative. I like that it won't cost too much. I like that we are focusing on an important issue."

The doubters among you may ask, "Why encourage an idea you do not like?" There are two reasons:

1) By emphasizing the part of the idea that you like, you might just redirect the person to refocus on that one part—and then come up with something good.

2) Encouraging people when they come up with a new idea helps create an atmosphere of possibility and innovation. By saying first what you like, the idea-giver feels heard and understood. She may think, "Well he likes part

of my idea." Even if this idea stinks, because she is encouraged she may come up with a good one tomorrow.

The first rule of LCS is always say what you like about the idea first. The second rule is to have a suggestion to go along with any concern you bring up. It can be a suggestion to deal with the concern or a suggestion to make the idea better.

For instance, "I like your idea because it is creative. I believe the workforce will buy into it and I believe it could solve the problem. However, it's not in the budget!" Now, *without* LCS the idea-generator is hung out to dry. The concern-maker has pointed out why it won't work and, unless the idea generator has an answer, the idea is dead. Checkmate!

However, by using LCS, the concern-maker is on the hot seat to respond to the concern. For instance, "My concern is that it is not in the budget, but why don't you ask Carl? Carl has a discretionary fund and maybe you can get the money from him." Or, "My concern is that it is not in the budget, but what if we use internal people for a pilot, instead of going outside, and then once we succeed, go after a budget for the rollout." Either way, you've stated your concern, but you've also given the idea-giver a suggestion of how to remove the concern.

With LCS, concerns are stated, but it feels like everyone is on the same side of the table. Instead of criticism, it feels like both sides are exploring how the idea can work, instead of engaging in a competition. Concerns *do* get stated. They just get sandwiched in between something you like and an answer about how to move it forward.

The results are unbelievably impressive. The atmosphere shifts. A positive feeling fills the room that wasn't there before. If you can get your people to buy into LCS, and follow its Likes, Concerns, Suggestions model, you'll see amazing ideas bloom, good ideas get better—and people feeling really great about the whole idea-generating process.

YOU ARE WHAT YOU EAT

A word about creative thinking and diet: Eating dairy and wheat taste great but will encourage a sorry sight of adult nappers in the afternoon. Likewise, heavy fare like pizza and Mexican food are energy killers. Not exactly what you want for creative brainstorming sessions!

Work with your clients to unobtrusively control what your participants eat during lunch. If they load up on carbs (pizza, pasta, pastries) you'll be lucky if they come up with ideas like, "Let's do a survey."

In Summary

When the Idea Eaters rain on everyone's parade:

- ➢ Move past limiting assumptions
- ➢ Make new neural connections
- ➢ Give feedback with LCS

Chapter 3:   The Tower of Vision: Reaching for the Moon

"If you can dream it, you can do it!"

-Walt Disney

> We've discovered how to regain the Roundtable of Collaboration and the Cauldron of Innovation. Now it is time to find our way back to the Tower of Vision, the place where an organization or team comes together around a common set of goals and values.

I'm an old strategic planner. A math major. When I learned to do strategic planning in the '70s professors hammered us to keep goals realistic. Now, these goals could be a stretch, but they had to be possible. Equally limiting, there was no heart or inspiration in the traditional planning model. Ahhh, but this strategic planning model was created before Neil Armstrong walked on the moon.

In 1961 John Kennedy astounded the world with his declaration, "We are going to put a man on the moon and bring him back safely by the end of the decade!"   In today's GPS-satellite-on-a-wristwatch world, that doesn't sound like a big deal. But in

1961, his bold vision was a shot heard 'round the world and heralded a new age. When I was growing up, my mother used to say to me, "Ben, you can no more do that than put a man on the moon." Putting a man on the moon was the epitome of the impossible.

In fact, immediately after Kennedy made his 1961 speech, the head of NASA approached the leader of the free world. "Mr. President," he said, "thank you so much for that speech. It's going to bring us millions of dollars as well as national and worldwide attention. But, I just want you to know— we haven't got a clue about how to do it. It's not on our radar screen. Maybe we can get an astronaut up there, but we sure don't know how to get him back."

President Kennedy did not respond with, "Well, that was just a political speech. Forget it." He also didn't say, "Well, let's just get the man up there and we'll worry about the rest later." Instead, he said boldly, "I know we don't know how to do that now, but I believe in NASA engineers' abilities to make it happen. I believe Americans can do anything we set our minds to do. So, we're going to hold this vision and get there by the end of the decade!"

The deadline was only eight and a half years away, and NASA hadn't even gotten started. Sounded impossible at the time, yes? No. Kennedy stuck to it, NASA employees were inspired, and the public cheered NASA on through the failures, the successes and the ultimate breakthroughs. *Astoundingly, the impossible happened just like he said it would.*

By casting the vision out ahead on a giant tether, then reeling it back in, step-by-step, NASA achieved breakthrough results. This is a stellar example of what the visioning model I will present to you looks like in the real world. You've witnessed the results of it with your own eyes: space travel, car travel, wireless computers, heart transplants, *etc.*

Visioning isn't just for presidents and space programs. Visioning is for companies who have hit a wall or are barreling towards one. Visioning is a critical tool today because markets are saturated, capital is drying up and margins are shrinking. Visioning helps organizations like yours exploit the value of their existing brands and staff.

For example, General Motors' sales were down. Employees brainstormed and came up with the idea of installing OnStar mobile information systems in new cars. Then, they saw the genius of breaking their own rules and made the system available to non-GM cars, to their competitors. Now OnStar is the industry standard—and a new large revenue stream for GM.

Take Starbucks Coffee. For decades upon decades, traditional coffee-makers thought they were selling ground beans. Then Starbucks broke the mold; it decided it was selling relaxation, an escape, a timeout experience infused with a better taste and a higher quality place to sip it. Now it seems you can't go a block without running into yet another Starbucks.

Visioning boldly declares. The framers of the Constitution didn't hang around waiting for instructions. They literally declared independence. Every time a couple says, "I do," or an umpire says, "You're out," someone is taking the risk to declare. Visioning—in organizations just like yours—shoots past the possible. Climb into the Tower, boldly declare your vision and be amazed at what can happen.

* * *

As we now take on Visioning, we must first confront the last two dreaded dragons that block the way to the Tower:

> - Chattering Monkey
> - Well-Meaning Weasel

The First "Drag on" Visioning: Chattering Monkey

"Progress involves risk. You can't steal second base and keep your foot on first."

-Fredrick Wilcox

Observable Symptoms:

- Tapping fingers, scribbling, nervous twitches and silence indicate that team members are resistant to full participation. Distracted by their internal concerns, they limit their investment in the process.

- Team members seem to have checked their hearts and humanity at the door. Present in body but not in spirit, participants are totally in their heads, unable to access their passion or compassion.

- Normal banter and humor is suppressed. Conversations are stilted. Participants act unnaturally serious in almost a caricature of "professional" behavior.

Have you ever looked around at a group gathered to do some work together and felt that sinking feeling? You know in your heart that you just don't have your team's attention. Their minds are elsewhere. You see people holding back, worried what others might think, unenthusiastic or clearly thinking one thing but saying another. As a facilitator or leader of a meeting or planning session this is enormously frustrating and hardly a great recipe for creating breakthroughs.

The culprit? Meet the "Chattering Monkey." This naysaying dragon has swung into the room, crouched by peoples' ears and is filling their heads with negative messages. And they are all over the place, wherever we go. Chattering Monkeys bully us internally, deadening our spirits and limiting our participation.

In this chapter, you will see how dangerous these pesky creatures can be and how to slay them. If a new, shared vision is to be unleashed, then facilitators must vanquish these dragons. Only then can the Genie come out to play.

What Happened to You Along the Way?

Imagine you are sitting in a seminar room with your co-workers. A man you don't know well is standing next to an empty chair. He picks up an intriguingly-shaped box, slowly leans in, scans the audience with his eyes, holds up the box and, in a loud stage-whisper, says:

"In this box I have something truly wonderful and amazing. (*You hear a faint drum roll or is it in your head?*) Who will be the lucky member of this group to snatch this prize from my hands? Who will take it home, show it to friends, and own this prize forever?"

The man waits for a moment, extending the pregnant pause. "Do you realize what I am saying? Only one of you will be offered this prize. . .and I'm going to give it to. . .the first person who jumps up and sits in this chair!"

Total silence. Not a muscle moves. A few nervous coughs (*who is this guy?*). After an excruciatingly long moment, someone finally does stands, walks up and sits in the chair. There is a loud sigh of relief and everyone laughs.

The stranger asks, "If this room were full of five-year-olds, what would have just happened? There isn't a five-year-old on the planet that, if I had used the same words with the same intonation, would not have lunged for the chair. Am I right?" he inquires.

Knowing smiles. Stirring. Nodding all around. "So, here's the $1 million question—since you were once five, too, what happened to *you* along the way?"

What Keeps You from Being Bold?

I have done this "experiment" hundreds of times and the results are always the same. Only one or two people will make a gesture toward the chair. The other people in the crowd don't even twitch. Do the same thing with children and every five-year-old will lunge for whatever chair is offered.

Research has shown that at five years old, we are at the height of our creativity, our curiosity and our willingness to trust both authority figures

> "Do not follow where the path may lead. Go, instead, where there is no path and leave a trail."
> - *Robert Frost*

as well as our playmates. Full of gusto, we are at the pinnacle of readiness to take risks and receive all that life offers.

But somewhere along the way, too soon after we are five, we stop grabbing for new opportunities. We begin to hold back and edit ourselves. Sometimes we just give up, resigned to a predictable, lackluster existence.

As adults, we are told to "get serious" about our lives, and we buy in big time. All that child-like verve and optimism is still a part of us—but instead of jumping up to grasp an opportunity, we sit back, skeptical and suspicious. "Yeah, like *which idiot actually believes* there is something inside the box?"

Yet. . .we still wonder about that darned box. We *want* to believe in mystery, to trust others, to get excited, to be our naturally bold, adventuresome selves. So our challenge now is to figure out a way back there.

Why The Chattering Monkeys Exist
Whenever we get the opportunity to reach beyond our comfort level, to step out and become all we can be, the mental dragons in our head start chattering, chastising and nagging: "Don't move! Don't leave this chair! You can't trust him. He's going to make a fool of you. Stay right there!"

Chattering Monkeys exist to protect us from harm, ridicule and loss. These are the voices in our heads that inhibit our natural impulse to do anything that might jeopardize the status quo. It is like static, interfering with our radio transmissions, keeping us from hearing the truly beautiful music. Chattering

Monkeys create a fog that prevents us from viewing a panorama. Wherever the Chattering Monkeys are present, we hold ourselves back and only offer what is safe.

So why do we allow this noise in our heads? Is something missing in us? The truth is we already have what we need to be brilliant. We don't need assertiveness training or personality profiling. We just need to quiet some of those Chattering Monkeys.

You will be amazed at the wisdom and inspiration that emerges when the monkeys are stifled. As a leader or trainer, your most important function is to *inspire* your team members to tap into their genius (or Free the Genie, to stay with our metaphor) for the good of your organization.

Here are some sure-fire ways to keep these Chattering Monkeys quiet.

Dragon Slayer #20: Move Them With Movement

The Chattering Monkeys just *lovvvvvve* to park somewhere, sit back and gossip. Add a desk or conference table and the chattering goes full bore.

So, as the leader or facilitator of a team effort, try to remove the tables and get everyone standing and moving as often as possible.

The Joy of Pacing

Did you ever hear of Seymour Cray? He invented the Cray Super Computer, which was revolutionary in its time. During the initial 18 months of development, he worked in the basement of his split-level house, which had a sliding glass door out to the backyard. There was a mound that covered most of the backyard.

Cray always kept a big spoon on his desk. As he worked on very difficult concepts, he would sometimes get stuck, hungering for a good idea. At those times he would stop, pick up his spoon, go out the sliding glass door and dig furiously into the mound. After a short while, he would have an idea to move him forward.

If he got stuck again, he'd run back out to the mound. He'd move—and then, BAM—get an idea. In the 18 months he was working on that project, he dug a tunnel into that mound almost across his whole yard—just from nervous, creative energy.

Here's a quick question to ask your group: "Are any pacers present here today?" *(It will get a laugh and invariably a few will have fun being "outed.")* Ask two or three pacers to pace and tell the rest of the group how moving helps them think. Encourage them to teach their sitting brethren how movement can get people unstuck.

Several Dragon Slayers already introduced do a good job of keeping people moving: Breaking into Small Groups, Carousel Brainstorming and Dot Voting. Go even further. Give participants the delicious permission to go outside the room to brainstorm and even to pop up and pace when the spirit moves them.

Movement inspires creativity. Get your people moving and they'll be more productive, resourceful and inspired.

No one knew this more than the Greek philosopher Aristotle. While in Athens, Aristotle founded an important school of philosophy, called the Lyceum School. The aristocrats of Athens said to Aristotle, "Let us build you a fine classroom inside a great building for your wonderful school of philosophy." But Aristotle would have none of it.

He said, "I don't want a room. Being cooped up in a building is not the best way to learn." Instead, when his students showed up in the mornings, they walked and talked with Aristotle—which is why the Lyceum School was also known as the Walking School. Aristotle knew there was something intrinsic to movement that was critical to creative thought, so he walked around the track all day with his students. As history has shown us, they came up with nothing short of the foundations for Western civilization. We, on the other hand, stick thirteen year-olds behind desks in rows and expect them to learn. Go figure!

Obviously, you and everyone else are going to be dizzy if you move non-stop, so I'm not saying start a walking school. I am advocating regularly building in movement to your planning meetings.

Dragon Slayer #21: Build in Mega-Fun

The third way to control the Chattering Monkeys is quite simply to laugh a lot. Laughter is the magic genie that lightens the energy and unites the group.

Invariably, the small groups that come up with the best ideas are the ones that are having a good time.

In the midst of the buffoonery, good ideas will pop up with surprising regularity.

That's because there is a documented, close scientific correlation between laughter's "Ha-ha" and inspiration's "Ahhhh-ha!"

Think about the beginning of a planning meeting. How do your participants enter in the morning? Aren't they often serious and stuck in their heads? A great time to use humor is right off the bat. Doing something fun and physical at the beginning of a session dramatically changes the way the rest of the meeting goes.

My favorite warm-up involves a time honored prop of circus clowns. As a metaphor for opening up and taking on new behaviors, I'll start a planning meeting by teaching people to juggle. It's physical. It's fun. It's a great status-equalizer. Best of all, it puts everyone into their bodies and invites their "inner child" into the session.

There are many physical group dynamic games and team challenges in the organizational development and human resources literature. Here are some of my time-tested favorites.

Gordian Knot

One of Hercules' Seven Trials was to untie the impossible "Gordian Knot." There is a quick, fun exercise by the same name which is a great team builder and energizer. It takes about ten minutes.

> "What we learn with pleasure, we never forget."
> - Louis Mercer

Here's how it works:

- Divide your group into teams of five to seven people.
- Each team stands in a tight circle facing one another.
- Everyone in the circle reaches out with their right arm and takes the forearm of someone in the circle who is not standing next to them.
- Then everyone reaches out with their left arm and takes the forearm of someone else in the circle who is not standing next to them; the Gordian Knot is now formed.
- The team challenge is to untangle the knot without breaking any of the arm connections (the arm connections can be twisted around but cannot be broken).

Unlike the original Gordian Knot, this is not a Herculean task—it can be done and it's a lot of fun getting there.

Calliope

As you know, a calliope bobs up and down. In the middle of a team session, especially right after lunch, bobbing up and down can really pick up the energy. In this exercise, participants are asked to sit on the edge of their seats while the leader reads a series of questions. The participants are told that when they hear a question or statement that applies to them, they should quickly stand up, look around and just as quickly sit back down again. It's fast, fun and clears everyone's brains.

Here are the kinds of questions that work well:

- Who's ever sent food back in a restaurant?
- Who here ever had an imaginary friend?
- Who has ever built a fort?
- Who's ever told off a sales clerk?
- Who gambles?
- Who's talked or cried their way out of a speeding ticket?
- Who's been proposed to and said, "no"?
- Who's said, "I love you," and didn't mean it?

- Who's ever played something other than a human being in a play. . .such as a tree or a rock or an animal?
- Who's ever sung a solo in front of an audience?
- Who sings in the shower? OK. . .Who sings every chance they get? *(At this point, I usually ask those standing to come up to the front and sing a song, to everyone's delight.)*

Cards

This is a fun, 20-second activity that can be used all day long. It's great to bring humor into the room, to re-focus attention or to reinforce desired behavior.

- Depending on the size of the group, buy two to five packs of playing cards and shuffle them together into one large pile.

- During the day, distribute cards for whatever you want to reinforce. For instance, a card to everyone who comes back from break on time, two cards when someone uses LCS, or three cards to each member of a small group that comes up with a particularly brilliant idea.

- After a break, ask everyone to look at the cards they have and get a "winner." (Winning changes at your whim: it could be whoever has the best poker hand, the most aces, the most spades, *etc.*)

- Award a small prize to the winner.

- Continue handing out cards and finding winners as the day goes on.

Dragon Slayer #22: Own Your Own Experience

If the meeting facilitator is in charge of each participant's attentiveness and energy, he or she is doomed to failure. Only the participants can control the Chattering Monkeys in their own heads. It is the facilitator's job to get them to own that responsibility. How? From the beginning, issue the challenge: they can make the session boring and worthless, or meaningful and powerful. The participants hold the key, not the facilitator.

Here is a perfect example. I was invited to a weekend on relationships. I didn't really want to do it, but one of my good friends kept pushing, so I finally gave in. My attitude was, "I know more than they do. They can't show me anything new!" So I stood on the sidelines all Friday night with another skeptic, and we rolled our eyes at all the exercises. Finally, late Saturday afternoon I had enough and left, cursing the waste of time and money.

As fate would have it, a year later my wife attended the same workshop (over my objections). She came back transformed and, although she didn't insist, sometime later she asked if I would consider taking the workshop again.

Much to my amazement, two years after I had taken the workshop for the first time, I found myself paying another $550 and. . .going again. However, this time I attended with a different mindset, determined to get my money's worth. I promised myself that I would get something important out of the experience and committed myself to remaining completely present throughout the workshop.

The workshop changed my life. It was one of the most powerful things I have ever experienced. Nothing changed from the first time. The facilitators were the same. The exercises were the same. The true value came from my decision to manage my own attitude and energy.

So at the beginning of every session that you lead, inspire your participants to take responsibility. You could say: *To make this day successful, you've got to be in this with me. Let's make this good. If it's not going well, say something. Tell me what needs to change. Don't roll your eyes with another skeptic. Don't wait until the end to complain. This is your company. It's your team. Take responsibility for YOUR own experience.*

Dragon Slayer #23: Help People Access Their Passion

Think about the amazing shift of mood that often takes place in that brief time before a planning meeting begins. Just before most sessions, companies usually serve refreshments at a table just outside or in the back of the meeting room. People stand around and talk like human beings, asking about each other's lives. Yet as soon as the meeting is called to order, people get serious and guarded.

They become cerebral and shut down their hearts— as if somehow this will show the boss what good employees they are. Yet what we want in an effective team meeting is the whole person, including the heart.

Quote Cards

One way of helping people get into their hearts right away is by using inspiring quote cards. I print them big, have them laminated, then post them on the walls. Some of my favorites can be found below.

"The best way to predict the future is to create it." – Peter Drucker	*"There is nothing permanent except change."* – Heraclitus
"Every act of creation is first of all an act of destruction." – Pablo Picasso	*"It's not as important where we stand, as in what direction we are moving."* – Oliver Wendell Holmes
"Vision is the art of seeing things invisible." – Jonathan Swift	*"Imagination is more important than knowledge."* – Albert Einstein
"You miss 100 percent of the shots you never take." – Wayne Gretzky	*"Without a deadline, baby, I wouldn't do nothin'."* – Duke Ellington

"Change your thoughts and you can change the world." – Norman Vincent Peale	*"A problem well-stated is a problem half solved."* – Charles Kettering
"If you insist on waiting for certainty, you will paralyze yourself." – J. P. Getty	*"Every child is born an artist. The problem is how to remain one once the child grows up."* – Pablo Picasso

An even more comprehensive list of inspirational quotes can be found in Addendum B of this book.

Before the meeting begins, ask participants to pick a quote that speaks to their heart. Start the session by having them read their quote to the group and say why it is meaningful to them. As people share, the atmosphere becomes more open and relaxed.

All-Too-Human Stories

This is a good technique to help the group remember that people are more than their jobs. Let's say you are about to enter a really intense meeting in which one group of people is angry with another faction. Change the atmosphere by asking them to start the meeting by standing in a "check-in" circle and sharing something in their personal life that they are really looking forward to. One person may begin by saying, "My only son is starting kindergarten." Another may say, "My wife just got a painting accepted in a gallery exhibit next month." Or "Our family is going on vacation at the shore next week." Suddenly there is lightness and a sense of human connection in the room.

Tom Brokaw Interview

Here's another way to make a human connection. Ask participants to turn to the person to their right and become Tom Brokaw for five minutes, ferreting out an interesting detail about that person's personality or life story. Then have the interviewer introduce their interviewee to the group in this way:

"You may think you know Fred, but did you know he. . .put himself through grad school driving a cab. . . grew up in Alaska. . .is an expert sushi chef. . .?

Getting people into their hearts is another way to tell the Chattering Monkeys to *put a sock in it.* When we tap into what we truly care about, we lose our self-consciousness. In the presence of our deep sincerity, other people around us also relax.

Music Makes the World Go Round

Music always changes the environment. It helps engage both sides of the brain simultaneously and re-engages the heart as the workshop ebbs and flows. It can take people back to when they were lighter and more fun. Music quiets Chattering Monkeys.

Music is also a terrific way to send people out and bring them back from breaks. Sometimes I tell meeting participants that anyone coming back from a break late will be expected to lead us all in singing karaoke.

I usually have some classical/ instrumental selection as background when small groups are working; pop and rock and roll to wake things up; inspirational music to accompany the group as it completes its work at the end the of day.

In Summary

If you want to throw the Chattering Monkeys off your team's scent:

- ➢ Move them with movement: Get them up and keep them moving
- ➢ Build in mega-fun exercises
- ➢ Challenge them to own their own personal experience
- ➢ Help them access their hearts and passion

The Second "Drag on" Visioning:
Well-Meaning Weasel

"Try? There is no try. There is only do or not do."

– Yoda

Observable Symptoms:

- Planning happens in silos, lacking a shared understanding or vision.

- No single person feels ultimately accountable for implementing projects and initiatives developed in the meeting.

- Follow-up meetings or reporting structures might be talked about, but nothing happens to insure that they really occur.

- Most efforts eventually trickle out or get lost in a corporate black hole.

The Well-Meaning Weasel slinks in when people file out from planning meetings. When I ask the question, "How did your planning meeting go?" the single most common answer I hear is, "Oh, we had a lot of ideas and we said we'd do a lot, but nothing was really different."

It is the same story repeated over again in businesses and other organizations. People leave meetings full of resolve to make changes and accomplish much. . .and nothing happens.

Even when there is a committee or a task force assigned to a project, people meet and talk about the initiative and then nothing happens. What's going on here?

It's like vowing to diet or start exercising. We know we should. We make firm commitments. We may develop specific strategies and regimens to get started. We might even invest money in our new initiatives. At first, when we are charged up and motivated, our intentions hold firm.

Then it's a downward spiral. We go back to our real, stressful, time-pressured lives and the regimen goes out the window. We miss a few steps, a few commitments and our motivation fizzles out. Soon our resolve is shaken. We create some rationalization and then go back to living our tolerably out-of-shape lives.

This is what happens to our resolve when we leave planning sessions. We start out fully committed and then the reality of our real, stressful, time-pressured job kicks in and we default to the same downward spiral of our old patterns.

It's not that there is some dastardly grand scheme to trip us up, or that people aren't well intentioned.

It's more like the temptation to let things "slip" is too great.

Picture some slippery weasel guy in a trench coat leaning against a lamppost in an alley, whispering, "Pssst, come here, buddy boy. What about your To Do lists? What about those emails you haven't answered? What are yah, nuts, taking something else on? *Ahhh, just let it go.*"

The Well-Meaning Weasel dragon lurks around the Tower of Vision *especially* when there is a planning session. So let's take a look at the Dragon Slayers that let us fight back.

Dragon Slayer #24: Craft a Vision Statement

This exercise quickly and powerfully creates alignment and direction, and focuses the planning process.

Throughout the 80s, crafting a vision statement meant eight-hour wordsmithing sessions in a conference room, where most everyone left exhausted and unfulfilled. No more. The following process allows a group to craft a unified, compelling vision statement in about 45 minutes. (*I should note that to do this you have to employ the "Can-you-live-with-it" consensus model, which is Dragon Slayer #5*).

Steps in Vision Statement Creation

1. ### *Wall Street Journal Role Play - Introduction*
   Small groups role play that it is five years from now and a Wall Street Journal reporter is here to find out about how this group has accomplished its vision over the past five years. Individuals talk about the highlights as though they have already happened — and have fun doing so.

2. ### *Individuals*
   Pass out file cards. Individuals work alone for 5-6 minutes to produce a vision statement for the team or organization, using 40 words or less.

3. ### *Small Groups*
   Individuals buddy-up. Each person reads his statement to his partner. The pair now puts their two statements together and comes up with a new statement that is 35 words or less. Now each pair comes together with one or two other pairs, into groups of four or six (depending on your total number of participants.)

   The hybrid statements are read and again the ideas are combined to come up with a small group statement that is only 30 words long. Keep doubling or tripling up and making the statements shorter until you have two or three statements on flip charts at the front of the room.

4. Large Group

For each flip chart vision statement, ask the other groups what they like best and circle those words and phrases.

Working on a blank flip chart, work with the whole group to craft a statement using the best of the best from the other charts.

5. Leave Unfinished

When the group is moderately satisfied say, "Okay, we are going to leave this now and come back to it at the end of the day. Is everyone okay saying this is a good working draft version of our vision statement?" (If you try to wordsmith to total consensus at this point, you run the risk of it taking hours.)

When you get that agreement, put the flip chart page that holds the vision statement on the wall and move on.

6. *Come Back Later*

Toward the end of the planning session, come back to this statement to do your final wordsmithing. You will find that people will be much more eager to put closure to it at this point. . .when they are exhausted and brain dead! My experience is that they truly will be happy with the statement and will not need to change it later.

A co-created, inspiring vision statement helps everyone stay on track as they move forward.

Dragon Slayer #25: Visionary Planning Grid

Planning processes frequently go off on tangents (called "rich conversation" by the people who create the detour). A lot of times no one but the facilitator knows exactly what the output is to be. And at the end of the day, the group has created 47 flip chart pages that will be typed up by someone who was not in the session, hopefully in a cogent order. Often not.

That's why I came up with the Visionary Planning grid. It combines the compelling inspiration of visioning with the specificity of planning, in a framework that is simple and very actionable.

This is one of the most powerful Dragon Slayers in this book. It effectively streamlines the visioning and planning process, while encouraging true understanding and engagement on the part of the participants. It is, in point of fact, the basis for my *Visionary Team Planning* process (see final chapter), which has changed how planning is done in many organizations.

This process can be completed alone, with another person, in a small group, a team or a whole organization. As you read through the description, refer to the "Visionary Planning Grid" on the next page.

As you see, the grid is divided into three parts: the *current reality* or how things stand right now; the *steps* of the plan; and the *vision* or desired results. Your planning will involve several categories. You will keep track of all of these on one piece of paper, using Post-it notes to fill in the categories as you do the planning process.

Note that you don't write directly on the grid, you write on small Post-its and stick them in place. This allows you to work back and forth between the whole picture and the details, and allows you to easily change it as time goes by.

VISIONARY PLANNING GRID

Key Results Areas	Current Reality	MILESTONES Projects/Initiatives			Year-end State	3-5 Year Vision

Note: For individuals, this grid can be made on 11"x17" paper with four or five rows such that the rectangle spaces are 1.5"x2", so that a standard small-sized Post-it Note fits in them. Use different color Post-it Notes on each line. For a team process use a 4'x12' wall mural with big Post-its or icons.

The piece of paper can be an 11" x 17" sheet of paper with one inch Post-it notes, for one or two people planning something pretty simple. It can be a huge wall-mural piece of paper on which you fit plate-sized Post-its, as 60 people are hammering out the future course for their organization for the next five years. It can be anything in-between. The process is the same, whatever the scope of the planning.

Steps in Creating A Visionary Planning Grid

1. **Determine the *"Key Result Areas"* (KRAs)** which are the things to focus on as you or your team/organization moves forward. In a business these KRAs could be: *Financial, Customer Service, Operational Excellence* and *People*. For an individual they could be: *Health, Work, Leisure,* and *Finances*. Whatever you choose, it is a good idea to keep the number of KRA categories to four, five or six.

   Write these KRAs on the Post-its and put them on the chart.

2. **For Each KRA, craft a** *"Current Reality Statement,"* **a** *"Year-end Results Statement"* **and a** *"3-5 year Vision Statement."* These have got to be general sound-bites, so be succinct, particularly on the vision statements. You'll get to be very specific later. Examples of these sound bites are:

- Current Reality Statements: "Going further in the hole every month," "Starting to take off," "In transition, with many new employees," or "Weak sales; flat growth."

- Year-end Results Statements: "Sales increased by 20%," "Key processes fully automated," "Employee recognition programs in place," or "Double-digit growth."

- 3-5 Year Vision Statements: "Zero defects," "People love working here: Employer of Choice." "We walk our talk," "Customers R Us,"

3. **For each KRA, determine the milestones** that will need to be reached in order to reach the *"Year-end Results Statement,"* and the *"3-5 Year Vision Statement."* These milestones are either the accomplishment of something significant

or the overcoming of an obstacle and are always written in the past tense with a verb at the end, *i.e.*, "Johnson grant application completed," "Four salespeople hired and trained," "New IT system researched and selected."

4. **For each milestone, brainstorm how you or your team/organization will achieve this milestone.** The "how" ideas will become the projects/initiatives to be worked on.

   (If you are an individual or very small group, this can be the end of this process. Now you will post your grid in a highly visible place to keep yourself clear about the priorities and time-lines for achieving your vision. If, however, you are using this grid in a team or organization-wide plan, you will also do the next two steps.)

5. **Determine who will drive each key project/initiative** (see Dragon Slayer #26 on the following pages, for more details on this concept.)

6. **Develop detailed action plans.** Once the grid (or wall mural) is completed, the individuals responsible for each project develop detailed action plan for completing their projects.

Using the Visionary Planning Grid as a Personal Planning Tool

I have most often used the grid in team planning sessions. In these cases, the grid turns into a large mural, taped on a wall on which the team planners glue pre-cut icons. However, the same model and steps can work well for individuals. By using a grid like the one shown on earlier in this chapter, individuals (or a small group of two or three) can sit together and create their own personal development, career planning or project plan.

I have also used it effectively in executive coaching or mentoring situations. The individual fills out the plan using standard small Post-it notes in various colors. Then he/she sits with a coach (executive coach, mentor or peer) and goes through the Post-its asking questions, receiving input and making changes.

Dragon Slayer #26: Crown a Champion for Each Initiative

A key aspect of success in a planning meeting is to determine a "champion" for each project or initiative. Before everyone leaves the meeting—and this is critical—ensure that ONE person (not two, three, or a committee) will oversee each initiative/project. A champion does not have to do all of the work. In fact, if the person can enroll others and delegate, he or she may not have to do much work at all. The champion is committed to keeping the idea/initiative alive and healthy, and to keep reporting the results back to a central group of champions.

As a point of illustration, you might want to remind the participants of one of the most famous corporate idea champions, Art Frye.

Sticky Ideas

Art Frye worked in the marketing department of the 3M Company about 30 years ago. One day a chemist came up to him and said, "Art, I've got a problem. You're a creative guy—maybe you can help me. We just mixed up a really big vat of adhesive for our tape and it doesn't stick well. It sticks for a second because it's a little tacky, but it peels off and it really isn't good for our tape." Art said, "Well, what do you want me to do?" "You're creative," the chemist said, "Maybe you could come up with some use for it." After serious thought he hit on an idea: what if it could be used on paper like a little bookmark, a little note or something. Art said to the chemist, "Well, put the stuff on little rectangle pads and bring them back up to me."

Then Art got so excited about this idea he told everybody he knew. Although his friends and relatives liked it, the head honchos at the 3M company passed. His boss, the Director of Marketing, was not impressed. The market research firm they used did not understand it. The advertising agency was horrified it might make 3M's slogan, "We make things that stick," a joke in the industry.

However, Art persisted so tenaciously that the company finally agreed to do a limited market test. The market test confirmed that the idea was worthless and would not sell.

But—this guy would not be denied. He tried everything…for months and months.

In a last ditch effort, he went up to the executive floor and gave all the secretaries the last batches of the pads and asked them to field test them. Two weeks later, the secretaries called asking for more and Art told them, "Oh, I'm sorry, I'm all out, you'll have to ask your boss." And they did. After a hurried meeting up on the executive floor, another market study was commissioned. This time the results were very different.

Today Post-it® Notes are the number one product of the 3M Company. Every month another color or shape comes out. This product has taken the company to new heights. Now, can you guess how much time passed between the time that that chemist walked into Art Frye's office and the time that they fully went to market? The answer is ten years! Art Frye wouldn't let that idea die for ten years.

Today, years later, Art Frye's picture is still on the wall at 3M!

Dragon Slayer #27: Set Up a Formal Tracking Structure

So now you have created a vision for your group, an organized Visionary Planning Grid, and engaged champions for each initiative. Yet there is another important step to ensuring accountability and keeping away the Well-Meaning Weasels. You need a Formal Tracking Structure.

This structure means post-planning session accountability meetings must be set up. These meetings are crucial or all the good work of the planning sessions will drift off into the ether and encourage another layer of employee cynicism. The post-session meetings will not only keep the energy of the meeting alive, they will also really impact the individual champion's motivation to keep working.

During the Meeting, Get Agreements:
- All champions agree to send finished action plans to a central resource within two weeks.

- All champions agree to meet within the next month to give one another feedback on their action plans and to report initial progress or problems that have arisen.

- The facilitator of the planning session (usually someone outside the organization or an internal change manager) agrees to come and psychologically hold the champions' feet to the fire.

- After the first follow-up, schedule these accountability meetings every six weeks. If a project is on plan, the champion need only report they are "on plan." If it is not on track, then the champion tells his peers what the problem is.

Expect this reality: most people still go back to their jobs and don't follow through on their commitments. Then two weeks before the next accountability meeting, they get some reminder e-mail and think, "Darn, that meeting is coming up. I'd better start doing something." (Actually, very few people say "Darn.") It's subtle, but the peer pressure works wonders, even better than a threat from a boss. No, things don't always happen as fast as everyone had hoped—but they *do* happen—and that's the idea now, isn't it?

When You Are Spread All Over the Country
Some of the companies I consult with schedule face-to-face check-in meetings every six weeks at various

locations across the country, in order to spread the travel commitments around. Others have opted for video conferences. Still others prefer live, real-time intranet conferences.

One Year Later

However they meet during the year, have the whole group get together again to share and celebrate what has been accomplished, update the plans and brainstorm new or enhanced projects for the coming year. Schedule these meetings one year after the initial planning session. Nothing beats a face-to-face meeting for re-energizing a group and encouraging the Genie to come out and play.

You'll be amazed what happens to your group over time. Working together to create and achieve an inspired vision is infectious. Even the most analytical groups get addicted. That's when excellent tools and processes turn into culture change.

In Summary

If you suspect that the Well-Meaning Weasel will show up and block your way to the Tower of Vision:

> ➢ Create a Vision Statement
> ➢ Use the Visionary Planning Grid
> ➢ Crown a Champion for Each Initiative
> ➢ Set up a Formal Tracking Structure

Chapter 4: Putting It All Together

So Now What?

You have identified the dragons and you now have 27 Dragon Slayers in your corner. So how do you apply them to the real world of your work? You can use each individually, a few at a time or all together in a comprehensive process called *Visionary Team Planning*.

1. Individual Dragon Slayers
   Obviously you can use any Dragon Slayer individually in any appropriate meeting where you believe it can make a difference. For instance, if Blah-blah Blob has rolled in and bloated your meetings or if the Chattering Monkeys have people locked into naysaying, suggest an exercise from one of those sections that knocks the dragon back on its heels.

2. Put Several Dragon Slayers Together
   You can put several of the Dragon Slayers together to create powerful team experiences.

   - Put the *collaboration* Dragon Slayers together and create an effective teambuilding session.

   - Put the *innovation* Dragon Slayers together for an innovation/ideation session.

- Put the *visioning* Dragon Slayers together and create an energized visioning and/or planning session.

I regularly use the teamwork and collaboration Dragon Slayers together in an intervention I call *"Building Team Trust and Effectiveness."* It really helps to clear the air and increase the team's performance.

I also put some of the team and innovation techniques together to create a program called *"Team Innovation,"* which helps teams tap into their collective genius in a short time and come up with breakthrough ideas. New product development teams particularly love these sessions.

3. But, if you really want to blow the top off your corporate or organization's culture, put *all* the Dragon Slayers together into the process called *"Visionary Team Planning."* When you master it, you will truly take your organization to a new level of possibility and effectiveness.

Visionary Team Planning: **Inspiration, Alignment and Action Plan in One Day**

Visionary Team Planning is a highly interactive, engaging process that allows individual departments, divisions, and/or whole companies to craft:

1) A unified vision of growth over the next 3-5 years

2) A 12-month aligned strategy

3) A detailed, tactical action plan that insures enrollment and accountability

There are three ways that this process is particularly powerful. It uses colorful icons and a wall mural to capture the excitement of the group's output, along the way inspiring every participant—from the most analytical to the most intuitive. It involves techniques, activities and language which let people at all levels of an organization work more easily with each other. The icing on the cake is fast turnaround. The whole process can often be done in only one full day.

The Map

A Visionary Team Planning wall map is a visually inspiring picture of where the team or organization is headed. If you want to see what the final product of a Visionary Team Planning (VTP) session looks like, just check out the internet.

You can see the finished product (map) in two ways:

1) You can go on my website: <chrysalis-consulting.com> to get a feel for what a session is like and how the map is constructed, or

2) Thanks to Raytheon Company and an e-learning outfit called E-change Solutions, finished VTP maps can now be put on the web for access by the people who created them. This is an amazing way of tracking and holding people accountable for the projects and initiatives they have agreed to champion. It allows everyone in the organization to log on to the internet to view and/or print out individual small scale versions of the plan. Further, because it can be updated, it ensures that the planning results stay alive.

The box on the next page describes in detail how to log on to this innovative site to view the tool and all it's features:

Accessing The Web-Tool

To view a demo of the web-tool and to see what a finished Visionary Team Planning map looks like, log onto: www.e-changesolutions.com/visionmap

- When prompted for your user ID, type in "demo." Type in "demo" for your password. Select "View A Map." Presto, you are in!

- To print the map, click on "Print 2"

- To view an Action Plan, click on the third yellow fish icon labeled, "Facilitators roadmap established," and then click "Progress Report."

- Finally, to review the progress-tracking feature, go back to the map and click on "Stoplight Chart" to the left of the map to see how the progress is being tracked. Note that overdue steps are under the red light. Steps due within 30 days are under the yellow light. Other current steps are green light.

Where VTP Has Worked Best

Putting all the Dragon Slayers into the Visionary Team Planning has been highly successful in a variety of organizational settings. Here are some key ones:

Advertising Agencies

Trying to get the people in creative departments or fields to involve themselves in planning is like pulling teeth. Trying to get them to commit to specific projects and timelines is difficult, and holding them accountable is a major headache. I ought to know. I was the CEO of an Ad Agency for eleven years. That's where the idea for this kind of planning got started. VTP is an extremely productive tool for getting the illusive, creative types actively invested in a planning process.

Analytical Organizations

Although first designed for "right-brained" thinkers, the overwhelming majority of the VTP work I have done has been with highly analytical organizations, like engineering organizations, actuaries, insurance companies, financial institutions, *etc.* VTP has proven to be great at getting people past their negativity and resistance. It is in these organizations where the effect of VTP on the culture has been the greatest.

Six Sigma

Visionary Team Planning cut its teeth working with Six Sigma Black Belts. For those unfamiliar, Six Sigma champions internal quality initiatives. Since 1995, I have worked with Six Sigma Black Belts from Texas Instruments, Motorola, Allied Signal, the Air Force, Kodak, Dupont, GE, Owens Corning, Raytheon and others, to bring this powerful process to their constituents.

Because the earliest sponsors of VTP were people from the Six Sigma community, the process was tailored early on to provide exactly what the Six Sigma Black Belts need. When Six Sigma is introduced into new cultures, it is often met with cynicism and resistance. VTP is a premier anti-resistance, pro-enrollment tool.

Six Sigma Black Belts are tasked with helping the organization/department "visualize" where they want to be. The VTP process takes visualizing to a new level! Many Six Sigma Black Belts are frustrated because they can't get their teams to generate potential target projects. The VTP has proven time and time again to help when nothing else works. Visionary Team Planning can be a significant tool in any Six Sigma Black Belt's tool kit.

Raytheon Company

If you want to find out the FULL potential VTP can have in an organization, contact Raytheon! They have embraced VTP with a vengeance.

It started in their Six Sigma groups and later spread to the Raytheon Learning Institute and Raytheon Professional Services. Ultimately, the company licensed the rights to the VTP technology, trained twenty of their Black Belts in facilitating VTP sessions and are teaching others to do so. They call their group the "VTP Navigators."

Thanks to the highly effective work of the Navigators and the company's active endorsement of the process, VTP sessions are almost daily at Raytheon. Many hundreds of Vision Maps have been created (they could make an "Atlas"). Carousel Brainstorming, LCS, "Can-you-live with it Consensus" and other VTP processes are now common terms at daily meetings of Raytheon's operating businesses.

Simply stated, it has changed Raytheon's culture.

VTP in Other Organizational Settings

The beauty of the VTP process is that it works for planning anything!

This has most often been used with the business community. Yet over 20 years, I have facilitated VTP sessions for wide-ranging and far-flung non-profit organizations. They include churches, retirement facilities, substance abuse agencies, public school districts, creative teams, private elementary schools, theatre groups, and a university that wanted to create a shared governance model between faculty and administration. Additionally, this works for individuals and families.

In all cases, reaching alignment was as important as producing the final Vision Map.

How To Do a VTP Yourself

If you are interested in leading a Visionary Team Planning session yourself, you will want to get the *"Visionary Team Planning Fieldbook,"* which contains a comprehensive facilitator's guide and other helpful items and information. Copies of this fieldbook are available through Chrysalis Publications at www.chrysalis-consulting.com or by calling 845-679-7072.

What Happened in Corporateland?

The Genie is Freed. . .So Now What?
In the Corporateland fairytale a brave band of leaders from the Kingdom employed the Dragon Slayers, slaying the dragons and freeing the Genie. Vitality came back to the three power centers as collaboration, innovation and visionary thinking abounded. And they all lived happily ever after.

In real life, it's not *quite* so simple. In real life the dragons are never really slain—only subdued. In real life the dragons hang around just out of sight, waiting for an opportunity to strike and imprison the Genie once again. . .and again. . .and again. So, in real life you have to remain conscious and vigilant.

Use the Dragon Slayers
Having read this book, you are now flanked by 27 Dragon Slayers to overcome the drag on your team's vitality.

Freeing the group genie and igniting the spark that helps them reach for the moon isn't serendipity or luck. Now you have a system. You, as leaders, trainers and change agents can have a pivotal role in revitalizing your organization, slaying the dragons and freeing the genie.

Nelson Mandela, the African activist who was imprisoned for 27 years, was elected president of his country when he was released from prison. Can you imagine — from prisoner to president! Mandela said, "Playing small doesn't serve the world. There's nothing enlightened about shrinking so others won't feel insecure. As we let our own light shine, we unconsciously give other people permission to shine. "

So be bold and you — yes, you — could free the genie that will help spark your organization to greatness!

APPENDICES

Addendum A: **Two Creative Thinking Techniques**

Addendum B: **Inspirational Quotes**

ADDENDUM A:
Two Creative Thinking Techniques

Here are two creative thinking techniques of the many I learned from Mitch Ditkoff at Idea Champions:

Creative Thinking Technique #1:
"Wish, Wild Wish, Fantasy"

In "Wish, Wild Wish, Fantasy" participants examine a question they are brainstorming and make a wish about it. Then someone else builds on it with a wish that is more far-out, and finally someone goes w-a-a-y out on a limb with an outrageous idea.

Here is an example of a group of individuals who built on each other's thinking and, by doing so, came up with a breakthrough idea. Some years ago, the Citibank Company had a big problem with long teller lines, as most banks did. If you tried to go to a bank on a Friday afternoon, you could hardly get into the bank. They couldn't hire people just to work on Friday afternoons even if they could find them because there was no place to put them. All the teller windows were already full.

One day, the bankers were sitting around grousing, "What the heck are we going to do about this?" Somebody said, "I wish everybody banked by mail. If everybody did that we wouldn't have a problem."

Somebody else chimed in, "You know what, we already know that everybody comes in with their paycheck. We know how much their paycheck is. We know how much money they want. They always come in at the same time. Why don't we just have appointments where we already know what they want and we do it ahead of time? So Joe Customer walks in at 2:30 PM and his packet with his deposit slip and his cash is ready. 'Hi, John, how are you doing this week?' says Marianne, as she hands John his packet. 'Fine, Marianne. Thank you, bye.' He's gone."

So by now the brainstorming has gotten wilder and they're all laughing.

"I've got something better than that," the next banker said, "Let's take a big cardboard box and throw a lot of cash into it and throw it out on the sidewalk. Anyone who wants to make a deposit, just throws more in. If anyone wants to make a withdrawal, they pull cash out." Of course, everybody laughed again.

Then someone else said, "Wait a minute, there are some good things about that idea. If we did the cardboard box it would be outside the bank, it would be operating 24/7, and customers would do it by themselves, so we wouldn't need a teller!" (There were a lot of other things that made it silly but this person was identifying the underlying principles—things that made the idea good: it's outside the bank, 24/7 and self-extraction).

You've probably figured out by now that's how the ATM machine was invented. They brainstormed the idea further, got it into production and created one of the all time killer apps, the first ATM machine.

Now it's time for you to employ the same kinds of creative thinking techniques that Citibank used. To help your people generate bold, new, impractical ideas—crazy ideas that will help them generate bold, new, practical ones—we'll use the technique called "Wish, Wild Wish, Fantasy."

How it Works
So let's say the question is "How can we understand the customer better?" You might start with, "Okay, somebody make a wish regarding this topic." Someone responds, "I wish every customer would just come tell us what they really want and

how we're doing." Now that's probably not going to happen, but it gets the ball rolling.

The next person has to up the ante. "I wish that we had a customer feedback mobile that looked like the bookmobile. It would drive around from customer to customer. Every customer would know that it would show up once a month and would be looking for it like the darn ice cream truck. He'd fly out his door all smiles, tell us his dreams and how we're doing as a vendor."

The next person has to stretch even more into the realm of fantasy. She says, "I wish we were all telepathic." The group laughs but then seriously asks, "What's the underlying principles behind being telepathic that would actually be good?" Someone answers, "We'd get all the information, real time, unfiltered from all the customers." Even though the fantasy ideas generated are impractical, they help the group focus on the parts of them that have benefit. Then the genie can take over and generate great ideas.

Then the group looks at their wish list and asks, "How else could we get all the information, real time, unfiltered, from all the customers?" Next, the group brainstorms ideas that will satisfy one or more of the underlying principles.

For instance, maybe someone says, "Perhaps we could have all the customers come into a room and we can have a 'What-If-We-Gave-You-Three-Wishes Customer Event.' It would be an event where they tell us what they like and what they don't like and what's on their radar screen that we should be thinking about."

Voila! Your team has come up with a practical idea based on the underlying principles derived from a fantasy idea. They've had fun. They've laughed. And come up with a good, bold, new idea. Not only does this technique give people permission to be wild they *must be wild* for it to work.

<u>Wish, Wild Wish, Fantasy</u>

- **WISH:** One team member expresses desire for successful outcome.

- **WILD WISH:** Build on this wish by stretching it further.

- **FANTASIZE:** Build on the third wild wish by stretching it way *beyond* the limits of possibility.

- **DISTILL** the fantasy by finding its underlying principles, the basic concepts hidden within it.

- **BRAINSTORM** the original question by using the underlying principles as triggers.

Creative Thinking Technique #2:
New Connections

If we are to be instigators of bold, new ideas, we must seize the ideas in the planning sessions we lead. Consider this illustrative story from the President of Sony. He was sitting on a park bench watching a guy listen to a boom box across the way. Then a jogger jogged by right in front—between him and the boom-box listener. This forced him to think of both things simultaneously—boom-box/jogger. In one split second the Sony Walkman was invented.

He wouldn't have thought of it if he didn't have both things in his vision at the very same time. Since we don't always have the benefit of that serendipity, we've got to create it in the sessions we lead. We've got to see jogger and boom box and make Walkman.

Let me give you another example from Colorado's main power company. For years, when the power lines froze in the Rockies the power company de-iced the power lines by expensive manpower. They kept power line workers holed up in a couple of cabins during winter. Every day these workers had to shimmy up the power lines and hit the power lines with big rods to shake the ice off.

This was an expensive, not to mention really boring, job with far too much downtime. As you might imagine, one day these workers were getting stir crazy in the cabins thinking, "This is terrible. It's the 20th century, for heaven's sake. There must be a better way of de-icing lines!"

One guy looked out the window as some squirrels were running across the power lines. "I've got it," he said. "Let's get squirrels up there and get them to run back and forth across the power lines to knock the ice off." Someone else said, "Yeah, right! Squirrels aren't big enough to knock the ice off. We need bears up there." "Ah-hah," said another, "and how are you going to get a bear up there, huh?"

"Honey! We go and put honey up there, the bear sees the honey, shimmies up the pole, swats at the honey, hits the power line and shakes the ice off." "Yeah, okay. And how are you going to get the honey up there?"

"Helicopters. That's it. We'll get helicopters to fly down low and hang buckets of honey from the power lines. The bears see them, shimmy up the poles, they swat at the honey and hit the power lines."

And while everyone was laughing hysterically, the team leader said, "Wait a minute, if helicopters came down that low, the downdraft from the helicopter propeller blade would shake all the ice off of the power line."

And today they get the ice off the power lines in the Colorado Rockies by helicopters. The cost of bringing in the helicopters is less than the cost of maintaining those guys in those cabins. The idea was brainstormed from squirrel to bear to honey to helicopter.

How it Works

The New Connections technique encourages everyone to do what the Sony president and the Colorado power line workers did by accident — connect two things together that previously were unconnected.

First the group free-associates a list of nouns that have nothing to do with the question they are about to brainstorm.

So if the problem is, "How can we improve the morale in this organization?" then the group starts with a noun that has nothing to do with improving morale. The first person might say, "circle." Then someone else says, "square." The next person says, "table," then "plate" and the last person says, "food." The group creates a string of words related to each other, but not to the question being brainstormed.

Now the first person has to take one of those words and come up with an idea to answer the question, even if it's a silly idea (and it usually is).

So here is how it might go if we are trying to come up with a way of improving morale using the words: circle, square, table, plate and food.

Person one says, "Okay, let's go into the cafeteria one day and have a major food fight. That ought to pep people up!" Now, the next person modifies the idea to make it more practical. He says, "Well, how about if we just give everybody a free lunch once a week?" The next person says, "That could be a little expensive. What if we had the free lunch day once a month?" The next person says, "What if we had a free lunch at a local restaurant once a month for the team that best exemplifies excellence and collaboration. You know we would foster a *spirit of pride* and healthy competition if we did that."

So they had a collaboration contest and recognition program. In a given month, the two teams that demonstrated the most cooperation and collaboration got to all eat lunch together for one week, complements of the company. This improved morale, teamwork and recognition.

There you have it. From table to square to circle to plate to food to a real idea. That's how New Connections works.

New Connections

- **FREE ASSOCIATE:** Building on and reacting to each other, the small team free associates a series of nouns totally unrelated to the problem at hand.

- **PICK A WORD:** One at a time each team member picks one of the unrelated words and tries to come up with an idea for the problem at hand using the word.

- **BUILD ON IDEA:** The next team member builds on, expands or improves the idea put forth by the first person.

- **CONTINUE PROCESS** until a good idea develops or if the process is stuck, then... begin again: Another person picks a different word from the list and starts the process all over.

- **STILL STUCK?** Make a whole new word list!

ADDENDUM B:
Inspirational Quotes

"The best way to predict the future is to create it."
– Peter Drucker

"If you can dream it, you can do it."
– Walt Disney

"Change your thoughts and you can change the world."
– Norman Vincent Peale

"Vision is the art of seeing things invisible."
– Jonathan Swift

"Imagination is more important than knowledge."
– Albert Einstein

"Most new ideas have a certain foolishness to them when first produced."
– A. N. Whitehead

"If you insist on waiting for certainty, you will paralyze yourself."
– J. P. Getty

"There is nothing permanent except change."
– Heraclitus

"Don't be afraid to take a big step when one is indicated. You can't cross a chasm in two small jumps."
— David Lloyd George

"A problem well-stated is a problem half solved."
— Charles Kettering

"The man with a new idea is a crank—until the idea succeeds."
— Mark Twain

"It's not as important where we stand, as in what direction we are moving."
— Oliver Wendell Holmes

"Be not afraid of growing slowly, be afraid of standing still."
— Chinese Proverb

"If you always do what you always did, you'll always get what you always got."
— Anonymous

"What I hear, I forget. What I see, I remember. What I do, I know."
— Confucius

"In the beginner's mind there are many possibilities; in the expert's mind there are few."
— Shunryu Suzuki

"Whether you believe you can or not, you're right."
— Henry Ford

"One of these days is none of these days."
— English Proverb

"What is now proved was once only imagined."
— William Blake

"To accomplish great things we must dream as well as act."
— Anatole France

"A pile of rocks stops being a rock pile when somebody looks at it with the idea of a cathedral in mind."
— Antoine Saint-Exupery

"Fall seven times, stand up eight."
— Japanese Proverb

"The way to get good ideas is to get lots of ideas and throw the bad ones away."
— Linus Pauling

"Without a deadline baby, I wouldn't do nothing."
— Duke Ellington

"Try? There is no try. There is only do or not do."
— Yoda

"You miss 100 percent of the shots you never take."
— Wayne Gretzky

"The biggest obstacle to learning anything is believing you already know it."
– Karl Albrecht

"A definition of insanity: doing the same thing over and over again in the same way and expecting different results."
– Rita Mae Brown

"The human spirit will not invest itself in a compromise."
– Robert Fritz

"Intuition will tell the thinking mind where to look next."
– Jonas Salk

"What we learn with pleasure we never forget."
– Louis Mercer

"Every child is an artist. The problem is how to remain an artist once the child grows up."
– Pablo Picasso

"Creative minds have always been known to survive any kind of bad training."
– Anna Freud

"The real voyage of discovery is not in seeking new landscapes, but in having new eyes."
– Marcel Proust

"Every act of creation is first of all an act of destruction."
– Pablo Picasso

"This ain't no time for slow ponies."
– Will Rogers

"You can't solve a problem with the same thinking that caused the problem in the first place."
– Albert Einstein

"Most of what we say and do is unnecessary—choose your words and actions wisely."
– Marcus Aurelius

"Over time, avoiding danger is no safer than outright exposure—Life is either a daring adventure or it is nothing!"
– Helen Keller

"If you keep your eyes focused on the financials—you can't see the customer."
– Bob Drewes

"For honor, not for honors. . ."
– Roman Proverb

"Hasten slowly"
– Roman Proverb

"Once the information you have is in the 40 to 70% range—go with your gut."
— Colin Powell

"I not only use the brains I have—I use all the brains I can borrow."
— Woodrow Wilson

"I tried to think, but nothing happened."
— Curly Howard

"With too much consistency a great soul has simply nothing to do."
— Ralph Waldo Emerson

"Never attribute to malice that which is easily explained by stupidity."
— Hanlon's Razor

"He who waits to do a great deal of good at once, will never do any good."
— Samuel Johnson

"Just do it!"
— Nike

"When you're finished changing—you're finished."
— Benjamin Franklin

"Strong convictions precede great actions!"
— J. F. Clarke

"My greatest concern is not whether you have failed, but if you are content with your failure."
– Abraham Lincoln

"Sooner or later, the man who wins is the man who thinks he can."
– Vince Lombardi

"A little rebellion now and then is a good thing."
– Thomas Jefferson

"I haven't failed. I just found 10,000 ways that didn't work."
– Thomas Edison

"The next section was going to be on the importance of flexibility and adaptability, but I don't have my slides, so I can't make the presentation."
– Training Specialist

"The journey of a thousand miles begins with a single step."
– Confucius

"I will find a way or make one."
– Hannibal (not the cannibal)

"Most people are about as happy as they make up their minds to be."
– Abraham Lincoln

"Never before in the history of man has the gap between what can be imagined and what can be accomplished been so narrow."
— Gary Hamel

"Mystery is the source of all true art and science. He who can no longer pause to wonder and stand rapt in awe is as good as dead."
— Albert Einstein

"Even if you're on the right track, you'll still get run over if you just sit there."
— Will Rogers

"If you're not fired with enthusiasm—you will be fired with enthusiasm!"
— Vince Lombardi

"I'd rather be a failure at something I love than a success at something I hate."
— George Burns

"Progress always involves risk. You can't steal second base and keep your foot on first."
— Fredrick Wilcox

"Man's mind, once stretched by a new idea, never regains its original dimensions."
— Oliver Wendell Holmes

"I count every day as wasted in which there has been no dancing."
— Friedrich Nietzche

"Changing culture is like moving a cemetery; you don't get much help from the residents."
— Anonymous

"The most bankrupt person in the world is one who has lost his enthusiasm."
— H. W. Arnold

"We must become the change we want to see."
— Mahatma Gandhi

"The price of greatness is responsibility."
— Winston Churchill

"Press on! Nothing in the world can take the place of persistence."
— Calvin Coolidge

"Yes, I like children, but I couldn't eat a whole one."
— W. C. Fields

"One must learn by doing; for though you think you know it, you have no certainty until you try."
— Sophocles

"Happiness lies in the joy of achievement and thrill of creative effort."
— Franklin Roosevelt

"You may be disappointed if you fail, but you are doomed if you don't try."
– Beverly Sills

"Tell a man he is brave, and you help him to become so."
– Thomas Carlyle

"A wise man will make more opportunities than he finds."
– Francis Bacon

"Doubt is a pain too lonely to know that faith is his twin brother."
– Khalil Gibran

"Leaders who never get carried away should be."
– Malcolm Forbes

"Never let yesterday use up today."
– Richard H. Nelson

"Trouble shared is trouble halved."
– Dorothy Sayers

"To be wronged is nothing unless you continue to remember it."
– Confucius

"Be like a postage stamp—stick to one thing until you get there."
– Josh Billings

"A man wrapped up in himself is a very small bundle."
— Benjamin Franklin

"If you want the rainbow, you gotta put up with the rain."
— Dolly Parton

"Problems are only opportunities in work clothes."
— Henry J. Kaiser

"A cynic is a man who, when he smells flowers, looks around for a coffin."
— H. L. Mencken

"I am not afraid of storms, for I am learning how to sail my ship."
— Louisa May Alcott